The Inclusive City

"Putting the 'inclusive city' on the agenda is an urgent task; it prompts us to address multiple exclusions too often encountered across urban areas. As such, this book provides a welcome antidote to the currently dominant technological efficiency of 'smart cities', by shifting the focus instead onto how we might define urban inclusion and encourage new policies and practices in its support."
—Simon Joss, Professor of Urban Futures, *University of Glasgow, Scotland*

"Inclusive growth is one of the most important ideas in the UN Sustainable Development Goals. Cities are the instances in which social and economic inclusion matters most. Martin de Jong and Ari-Veikko Anttiroiko, both known scholars in the field of urban planning, have written a most compelling book on inclusive cities. They show that economic inclusion should be given a high priority in the making of an inclusive city."
—Shunsuke Managi, Distinguished Professor and Director of the Urban Institute at *Kyushu University, Japan*, and Director of UNEP Inclusive Wealth Report

Ari-Veikko Anttiroiko • Martin de Jong

The Inclusive City

The Theory and Practice of Creating Shared
Urban Prosperity

Ari-Veikko Anttiroiko
Tampere University
Tampere, Finland

Martin de Jong
Erasmus Initiative for the Dynamics
of Inclusive Prosperity
Erasmus University Rotterdam
Rotterdam, The Netherlands

ISBN 978-3-030-61364-8   ISBN 978-3-030-61365-5   (eBook)
https://doi.org/10.1007/978-3-030-61365-5

This Palgrave Pivot imprint is published by the registered company Springer Nature Switzerland AG.
The registered company address is: Gewerbestrasse 11, 6330 Cham, Switzerland

Acknowledgments

We would like to express our great appreciation to all those colleagues who have helped us with this book project. Ari-Veikko Anttiroiko expresses special thanks to Tampere University, and Martin de Jong wishes to thank the Erasmus University Rotterdam and more specifically the Erasmus Initiative for the Dynamics of Inclusive Prosperity.

CONTENTS

ABOUT THE AUTHORS

Ari-Veikko Anttiroiko is an Adjunct Professor at Tampere University, Finland. His main research areas include local governance, local economic development, and public-sector innovations. He has edited several internationally distributed books, including *The Political Economy of City Branding* (2014) and *New Urban Management* (Palgrave Macmillan 2015).

Martin de Jong is Scientific Director of the Erasmus Initiative for the Dynamics of Inclusive Prosperity and Professor at Erasmus University Rotterdam, the Netherlands. He has published books and a variety of journal articles in the fields of urban and transport infrastructure development and public administration, especially on China.

LIST OF FIGURES

LIST OF TABLES

CHAPTER 1

Introduction

Abstract The dominance of the techno-economic paradigm in urban development has laid bare major socio-economic problems in city, of which the growing inequality is not the least. Much of the literature on inclusion and the inclusive city emphasizes the need for social inclusion to remedy these problems. Chapter 1 discusses the premises of inclusive urban development and highlights the importance of economic inclusion and the need to utilize people's capabilities and assets in resource integration and value creation in the city. The last section of this chapter outlines the structure of the book.

Keywords City • Urban development • Social inclusion • Economic inclusion • Inclusive prosperity • Value creation

THE CITY IN FOCUS

Cities are dense urban settlements that have become the epitome of modernity, development, and economic prosperity. They have been described as one of the humankind's greatest social innovations and are arguably a fundamental precondition for improving the material and immaterial conditions of people's lives (Glaeser, 2011). This holds true in particular for cities in the developed world, that is, cities in wealthy

© The Author(s) 2020
A.-V. Anttiroiko, M. de Jong, *The Inclusive City*,
https://doi.org/10.1007/978-3-030-61365-5_1

countries with post-industrial economies, technologically advanced infrastructures, and institutions needed to sustain democracy.

However, even if cities have helped us grow richer, smarter, greener, healthier, and happier, as claimed by Edward Glaeser (2011), their rise has not been without challenges and contradictions. Many scenarios portraying our urban future demonstrate risks and dangers resulting from technological development, environmental problems, public health issues, instability due to socio-economic inequality, and external threats such as those exacerbated by global climate change.

Due to a profound transformation in the techno-economic paradigm which evolved in the post-war decades, it has become a major challenge for cities to adjust to changing conditions in the global digital age (Sassen, 2010). Accelerated scientific development resulting in various high-tech applications has led urban governments and communities to emphasize the role of technological solutions in solving urban problems, as reflected in the rise of smart city discourse (Komninos, 2015). On the other hand, a matter not to be overlooked when considering urban development is that even if the physical infrastructures, facilities, and applications in urban technology are essential for the functioning of the city, its soul lies in human interaction. Innovativeness, creativity, entrepreneurship, revitalization, and resilience of urban communities rest primarily on the *social nexus*. While fairly recent discussions ranging from the productive role of social capital to the stabilizing impact of inclusive prosperity increase our understanding of this social nexus, there is still a lot to learn about the social dimension of urban development.

BALANCING SOCIAL AND ECONOMIC DEVELOPMENT

The social dimension of urban development invites us to consider how human and social potential in the pursuit of urban development can be strengthened. This challenge is often referred to as the social agenda or more broadly as social sustainability (Baldwin & King, 2018). Such an approach often tends to focus primarily on social problems such as poverty, inequality, and exclusion, while downplaying the need to secure preconditions for productivity, innovativeness, and long-term growth. Such an orientation generates problems in times of global competition and makes the provision of welfare and well-being for large segments of society unattainable. The need to balance sound economics with social equity and stability urges us to reconsider central premises underlying public policy, at both national and local levels.

Local governments tend to suffer from a lack of resources to further their urban development. It is therefore worthwhile examining how cities could better enhance their ability to benefit from having local stakeholders on board and let them contribute to inclusive prosperity. This would imply creating conditions for the optimal utilization of human capital, social capital, and various other forms of capital available in urban communities. A concept encapsulating this discussion is *inclusion*. Our hypothesis is that while inclusion is conventionally seen as a policy challenge motivated by human rights, equality, and justice, it has in fact tremendous potential as a morally more neutral strategic concept to foster urban social and economic development in a broader sense.

While decade-long global economic growth has lifted millions of people out of poverty, our world has also reached unprecedented levels of income and wealth disparity in that same period. Consequently, wealth is held by a tiny minority of the people and large segments of the population have been left behind. In such a situation, issues related to inclusion, sharing, and solidarity are bound to become critical. Discussions about inclusive capitalism (Green, 2017; Jacobs & Mazzucato, 2016), inclusive prosperity (Naidu, Rodrik, & Zucman, 2019), and inclusive growth (Lee, 2019) are signs of such concerns. The *inclusive city* is a development-oriented policy concept that can play an important role in adducing a social perspective to the promotion of economic development and, reversely, an economic perspective on social development.

We contend that the idea of social inclusion should be more than merely fixing the perverse outcomes and exclusionary practices of instrumental neoliberal approaches to the promotion of urban growth. We make a plea for a new urban socio-economic model in which a fine balance is struck between the social and the economic dimensions of urban development. This can be done by making both value creation and consumption inclusive and accounting for the contributions that various types of capital (human, social, physical, and natural alongside financial) make to trigger economic development. The above line of thought paves the way to redefine public policies, including measurement that goes beyond GDP alone, commitment to building competitiveness through broad-based utilization of various capabilities existing within the urban community, democratization of innovation, the building of sharing institutions, and reliance on ecological modernization, just to name a few aspects of this new paradigm for socio-economic development (cf. Aiginger, 2014).

Toward Inclusive Urban Development

In this volume, we will provide conceptual tools for understanding and designing shared prosperity in cities. The foundation of the conventional idea of an *inclusive city* is a democratically governed citizen-centric urban community with a high degree of sensitivity to social issues (Hambleton, 2015). The historical roots of such a progressive view grew primarily in the developed world in the nineteenth and twentieth centuries as a response to various drastic forms of social and economic exclusion. The post-war decades witnessed the rise of increasingly diverse metropolitan cities in terms of social class, ethnicity, language, religion, lifestyle, gender identity, and a host of other features.

The inclusion of societal groups representing such a variety in capabilities provides enormous economic potential. However, building an inclusive city is a complex exercise, both intellectually and politically: intellectually, because it comprises a host of different dimensions sometimes leading to contradictory requirements and situations; and politically, because the policymaking, governance, and management of inclusion-oriented urban development processes should take stock of stakeholder interests that are not always easy to accommodate.

The idea of inclusion is not as self-evident as it may appear at first sight. It is often quite manageable to address the inclusion of a particular disadvantaged group and assume the benefits of such an action. But it is much more demanding to comprehend the big picture of social inclusion in terms of complex intersectional relations in the urban context, not to speak of building an agenda in which this multifaceted set of well-intentioned actions is turned into a source of urban value creation. Thus, inclusion should not be confined only to disadvantaged or marginalized groups, but also cover groups not usually taken into account in inclusionary policies, such as families with children, students of local educational institutions, senior citizens, customers of a particular hospital, and non-credit card holders, depending in each case on the community characteristics, historical context, identified potentials, and development goals.

The power of inclusion becomes evident when, for example, students are openly invited to contribute to innovation processes initiated by local firms in a facilitated student-involving platform, as is the case with Demola in Tampere, Finland. Without such a strategically motivated inclusion the potential of 40,000 higher education students in this mid-sized post-industrial city would have simply been left underutilized. The same kind of potential can be associated with new channels for senior, academic, or ethnic entrepreneurship, crowdfunding for community-based projects, or business ideas for parents at home. Similarly, mixing urban functions, improving public transport, and promoting community safety can increase inclusion with the potential to enhance interaction, communication, and entrepreneurship. Examples like these can offer practically endless possibilities for various segments in the urban community to harness and contribute to socio-economic development.

To sum up, this book builds up a comprehensive conceptual framework for understanding inclusive urban development. It discusses how various aspects of inclusion contribute to urban development; demonstrates how value trade-offs may occasionally be deemed necessary when policymakers promote social, economic, and political inclusion; and examines the governance issues related to such an endeavor. Toward the end of the book, we use the examples of four cities from both sides of the Atlantic to illustrate different conditions of and strategic approaches to the promotion of the inclusive city.

Our central assumption is that multidimensional urban inclusion is not merely a precondition for the promotion of equity, justice, broad accessibility to public services, and well-being for all, but also an opportunity to widen the local resource base, create collaborative synergies, improve conditions for entrepreneurship, and boost public value creation. In short, it is designed to widen the group of people involved in and contributing to local value creation.

STRUCTURE OF THE BOOK

Following this introductory section, in Chap. 2 we will focus on changes in and challenges to the urban development paradigm. What made previously dominant business-oriented and neoliberal approaches to urban development fail to live up to their promise and which alternative approaches and city labels appeared in the past few decades in their stead? And with the inclusive city figuring among them, what are its main features and associations in the development discourse? Our next step in Chap. 3 is then to map the broader conceptual field surrounding "inclusion" with its various ethical aspects, followed in Chap. 4 by a deeper analytical operationalization of the various grounds used for excluding individual and social groups from various types of capital in the city. This sheds light on what the realization of an inclusive city looks like and which trade-offs this requires. In Chap. 5, we move on to highlight the transition from a rights-oriented view toward an entrepreneurial and co-creation-oriented perspective of urban prosperity, that is, prosperity produced and shared by community members with variegated backgrounds, capabilities, and positions. After addressing the policy agenda for realizing inclusive urban prosperity, we will outline its planning and governance in Chap. 6. We pay special attention to the orchestration of stakeholder interests for the benefit of inclusive urban prosperity. The above theoretical debates are then empirically concretized in Chap. 7, which collects descriptions of real-life initiatives toward realizing the inclusive city in Europe and North America, with a focus on Helsinki, Barcelona, Portland, and Pittsburgh. In the last section of the book, we will summarize the idea of the inclusive city and highlight our general policy recommendations for politicians, urban managers, and local stakeholders aiming to transition in that direction.

References

Aiginger, K. (2014, June). Industrial Policy for a Sustainable Growth Path. WWW for Europe Policy Paper, no 13. Retrieved November 1, 2019, from http://www.oecd.org/economy/Industrial-Policy-for-a-sustainable-growth-path.pdf

Baldwin, C., & King, R. (2018). *Social Sustainability, Climate Resilience and Community-Based Urban Development: What About the People?* London: Routledge.

Glaeser, E. (2011). *Triumph of the City: How Our Greatest Invention Makes Us Richer, Smarter, Greener, Healthier and Happier.* New York: Penguin.

Green, D. (2017). *Inclusive Capitalism: How We Can Make Independence Work for Everyone.* London: Civitas.

Hambleton, R. (2015). *Leading the Inclusive City: Place-based Innovation for a Bounded Planet.* Bristol, UK: Policy Press.

Jacobs, M., & Mazzucato, M. (Eds.). (2016). *Rethinking Capitalism: Economics and Policy for Sustainable and Inclusive Growth.* Chichester, UK: Wiley-Blackwell.

Komninos, N. (2015). *The Age of Intelligent Cities: Smart Environments and Innovation-for-all Strategies.* London and New York: Routledge.

Lee, N. (2019). Inclusive Growth in Cities: A Sympathetic Critique. *Regional Studies, 53*(3), 424–434. https://doi.org/10.1080/00343404.2018.1476753

Naidu, S., Rodrik, D., & Zucman, G. (2019, January). Economics for Inclusive Prosperity: An Introduction. *EfIP Research Brief*, January 2019. Economists for Inclusive Prosperity. Retrieved October 31, 2019, from https://econfip.org/wp-content/uploads/2019/02/1.Economics-for-Inclusive-Prosperity-An-Introduction.pdf

Sassen, S. (2010). Reading the City in a Global Digital Age: The Limits of Topographic Representation. *Procedia—Social and Behavioral Sciences, 2*(5), 7030–7041.

CHAPTER 2

Pinpointing the Urban Paradigm Shift

Abstract From the 1980s on, a techno-economic paradigm for urban development has encouraged local governments to promote policy agendas that reflect the idea of neoliberal city. This approach has been popular until the 2010s. More recently, however, it has faced growing criticism for contributing to widening divide between haves and have-nots. A thorough analysis in the use of city labels demonstrates that city labels usually aligned with neoliberalism, such as competitive city, entrepreneurial city, creative city, and knowledge city, are contested on good grounds, while the use of socially oriented and "softer" ones, such as inclusive city, sharing city, and safe city, seems to be rising. This chapter concludes that realizing the inclusive city requires that special attention is paid to social aspects of urban development, while reminding that occasionally value trade-offs between different groups and interests may be unavoidable.

Keywords Neoliberal city • Urban divide • City label • Inclusive city • Value trade-off

THE NEOLIBERAL CITY: FROM COOL TO COLD

Since the beginning of the twenty-first century, an ever-widening array of academics has addressed the damaging impact of "raw capitalism" and neoliberalism in socio-economic policies in general and urban governance in particular. The presence of market forces in the provision of public

© The Author(s) 2020   9
A.-V. Anttiroiko, M. de Jong, *The Inclusive City*,
https://doi.org/10.1007/978-3-030-61365-5_2

services and an exclusive orientation toward profit-maximization and cost savings has been seen to undermine the social fabric in cities. Hambleton (2015), for instance, calls for civic leadership among those responsible for urban governance to counter the influence of faceless global private-sector leaders who have the narrow financial self-interest of their multinational corporations in view rather than the interests of place-based communities. Actually, a great many authors have expressed reservations or even dismay at neoliberal policies leading to growing divisions between haves and have-nots within cities, with the former driving the latter because of rising shortage in affordable homes, especially in attractive neighborhoods (Mayer, 2017; Pinson & Morel Journel, 2017; Storper, 2016; Van Eijk, 2010). Changing tides in both the ideological landscape and public policies at different levels suggest that the neoliberal era is coming to an end.

Let us start by shedding light on the recent historical context of the transformation of the urban paradigm, epitomized by the gradual loss of appeal of neoliberal city labels such as the competitive city, the entrepreneurial city, and the creative city. The post-World War II period witnessed an unparalleled economic growth, which not only benefited the USA and Western Europe but also started a process that drew millions of people out of poverty, especially in Asia. This is known as the golden age of capitalism, which was paralleled by a gradual rise of welfare societies in the developed world. At that time, many countries witnessed an improvement in socio-economic equality (as evidenced in Gini index scores), a rise in the impact governments had on national and urban economies, and the emergence and expansion of a variety of social services in the welfare state. The 1970s and the first half of the 1980s saw the culmination of this public-sector project.

In the wake of economic recessions and decreasing confidence in the effectiveness of public-sector operations, financial stringency led to a step-by-step retrenchment of the welfare state and its accompanying institutional arrangements. In lockstep with this development, the status of corporations and entrepreneurs began to grow again alongside the preparedness of national and urban governments to accommodate their policy claims, wishes for attractive spaces, and favorable conditions vis-à-vis taxation. The collapse of socialist states and the fall of the Berlin Wall in 1989 symbolized the bankruptcy of many left-wing ideals and were not just considered by many as evidence that socialism had faltered but also that neoliberalism was on the right side of history at least with regard to economic issues.

This was the time of economic globalization, technological progress, and increased importance of global instrumental networks. These certainly amplified economic growth, but also contributed to the emergence of alarming trends, such as the signs of "great decoupling" (Brynjolfsson & McAfee, 2014). In short, economic growth no longer increased employment or median household income as it used to in the previous decades, but instead began to increase within-country inequalities and urban poverty even in the most advanced economies. This development went hand in glove with an entrepreneurial perspective of cities and urban development. The city had to be entrepreneurial, competitive, and creative to ensure that the right companies in high-tech and advanced producer service industries and the most talented people were attracted to it.

This idea was eloquently described in Richard Florida's *The Rise of the Creative Class* (Florida, 2002), in which he pointed out that the classical distinction between capitalist and working classes (which had prevailed in industrial times) had long been supplemented by the new creative and service classes, which were both tied to the service industries and had superseded extractive and manufacturing industries in many cities. While the service class was composed of vulnerable employees with limited professional training reliant on temporary contracts and whose labor was essentially interchangeable with that of others, members of the creative class had followed more specialized education pathways and offered qualifications at the labor market, which were either in high demand or hard to substitute or even both. Since representatives of the creative class generally earned more, were employed by corporations with higher value added and less visible negative impact on the physical environment, and lived more often in high-brow private dwellings, their contribution to the municipal coffers was far more impressive as well. It was therefore especially the members of the capitalist and creative classes, which urban governments were eager to attract, while members of the working and service classes were both less desirable and easier to lure into the city if needed for the local labor market.

The lasting dominance of this business approach to urban affairs, however, did result in a gradual weakening or even dismantling of the previously hailed welfare state. It also led to the elimination of many of its institutional arrangements that had possibly weakened the flexibility and entrepreneurial spirit of its companies and residents, but also served to protect underprivileged families and individuals from sinking into lasting poverty and apathy. While many large corporations and small high-tech start-ups were celebrating impressive profits adding handsome dividends to their owners and managers, the Gini index of nearly all countries and cities began to show marked increases again (the Gini index or coefficient is used to measure inequality). Intriguingly, Florida's more recent work entitled *The New Urban Crisis* (Florida, 2017) reflects this particular trend: while staying with his points made earlier regarding the growing size and influence of the creative class and its visibility in the urban texture, his evaluative assessment of it changed. Given their higher income, they have over time been able to collect real estate in most American and European cities at the more central and appealing locations in the city, driving out members of the working and service classes to neighborhoods in the suburbs or even out of town. Urban segregation was beginning to be felt in many cities—at least in the Western world and particularly so in North America.

The urban divide proves to be particularly marked in the economically successful cities where high-tech and other advanced professional services show a strong presence. In other words, urban economic developments are taking us further and further away from *inclusive urban development* rather than closer to that ideal. Although the interpretation of what "neoliberal" entails appears to differ from author to author and from one national and local institutional context to another, the ideological portée of the message for many contemporary critics is clear: neoliberal economic policies have made cities increasingly *exclusive*. It is perhaps more than a mere coincidence that the fall from grace of the neoliberal city evolves while the Anglo-Saxon private-sector model of capitalism known as the Washington consensus faces mounting international opposition and shriveling credibility. To be neoliberal was modern and cool in the 1980s, but it is widely regarded as irresponsible and outdated and cold in the 2020s.

FROM SUSTAINABLE THROUGH SMART TO INCLUSIVE CITIES?

A particular novelty in urban governance largely connected with the entrepreneurial attitude that emerged around the 1980s was the application of marketing strategies and tactics to lure investors, residents, and visitors into cities. This started out as city promotion, relatively basic self-advertising primarily for the purpose of enhancing one's reputation as a tourist destination, but then gradually matured into city marketing through the adoption of more sophisticated tools to collect information from and distribute information to target audiences. More recently, it evolved into fully fleshed city branding (Anttiroiko, 2014; Ma, Schraven, de Bruijne, de Jong, & Lu, 2019). Apart from adopting city brand identities specific to their own situation aimed at providing a description of how they wish the outside world to see them, they have also increasingly frequently used a variety of city categories or labels. These city labels tend to reflect the economic or industrial profiles cities wish to adopt and/or convey of themselves, ranging from sustainable city through smart city to inclusive city and many more. The most popular city labels as identified in the academic literature are presented in Table 2.1.

De Jong, Joss, Schraven, Zhan, and Weijnen (2015) conducted an initial bibliometric study in which they examined the use and conceptual association of 12 different city labels during the years 1996–2015, which was replicated and further refined for 35 different city labels for the period 1990–2019 (Schraven et al., 2020). Their studies are intriguing, since they place the emergence and rise of the label "*inclusive city*" in the context of a large number of other labels. The findings demonstrate that the *sustainable city* label has been the most commonly used for many of the years under study, primarily because it is an umbrella category comprised of both social, economic, and environmental policy agendas (see Joss, 2015). They also found that it was more strongly connected to other environmental labels such as *compact city, eco city, low-carbon city, green city, resilient city, sponge city,* and *circular city,* which occurred less frequently and could therefore be regarded as satellite labels in an "eco cluster." The *smart city,* on the other hand, appeared much later in the time-frame under investigation, and demonstrates a far stronger affinity with the *digital city,* the *virtual city,* the *future city,* the *intelligent city,* the *ubiquitous city,* the *connected city,* and the *information city,* which all provided conceptual ammunition to but eventually ceded their place to their far more impactful and versatile nephew, the smart city. The smart city has over time become the leading figure in what can be considered a "techno cluster" of city labels. The reasons for the growing popularity of the smart city were very similar to those leading to the dominance of the sustainable city label in the other cluster: the capacity to absorb general insights and viewpoints from other labels and act as general, more popular umbrella concept. Apart from these two clusters, a number of relevant other city labels display significant scores (though not nearly as much as the sustainable and the smart), such as the *creative city,* the *knowledge city,* the *entrepreneurial* city, the *competitive city, knowledge city,* and the *learning city,* which were already of older origin and focused on the attraction of

Table 2.1 List of 35 most popular city labels in the academic literature 1990–2019

Rank	City concept	No. of articles
1	Smart city	5161
2	Sustainable city	1753
3	Compact city	671
4	Creative city	529
5	Eco city	458
6	Future city	410
7	Green city	364
8	Digital city	304
9	Low-carbon city	301
10	Resilient city	273
11	Virtual city	255
12	Sponge city	237
13	Livable city	235
14	Open city	162
15	Knowledge city	157
16	Safe city	112
17	Intelligent city	109
18	Entrepreneurial city	109
19	Circular city	91
20	Inclusive city	91
21	Competitive city	76
22	Connected city	71
23	Ubiquitous city	53
24	Learning city	49
25	Solar city	48
26	Information city	28
27	Sharing city	23
28	Productive city	19
29	Zero-carbon city	17
30	Post-carbon city	15
31	Biophilic city	13
32	Experimental city	12
33	Regenerative city	11
34	Playful city	4
35	Renewable city	4

Source: Modified from Schraven, Joss, and de Jong (2020)

high-tech industries and creative minds, much in line with the neoliberal agenda referred to above. But very interestingly from a perspective of the newly emerging social agenda in urban development, the most recent trend in the time-frame 2014–2019 leads to two more staggering conclusions.

- From 2013 on, the smart city label has skyrocketed, eclipsed all others, and even overtaken the sustainable city in numbers of references in the academic literature. The most likely reason for this success is that governments, the real estate sector, and large engineering corporations can join forces and actually construct ICT and Internet of Things-based neighborhoods, infrastructures, and facilities and present them as a fruitful compromise between economic interests (they are aimed at economic growth and can be made profitable), environmental interests (digital industries are believed to be more environmentally friendly than most forms of manufacturing), and social interests (online use of smart services can be opened to the broader public and theoretically allow them to engage in more open interaction with governments and providers). Many members of the eco city label cluster tend to be mentioned frequently in policy documents, but it is far harder to transform them into appealing business models with which attractive financial revenues can be generated for governments and corporations.
- During the second half of the 2010s, in addition to the staggering rise of the smart city, the findings in the study point at the rise of a few new city labels, which can neither be strongly associated with the labels within eco cluster nor with those in the techno cluster. Most prominent among them are the *open city*, the *safe city*, the *inclusive city*, and the *sharing city*. Apart from them being fairly recent in entering the scene, one could also surmise that they seem to usher in new conceptual associations and a new type of intellectual policy agenda for cities which is not environmental, corporate, or technology-driven: it in fact centers around social issues in the city. It would be premature to call the burgeoning of these labels as the rise of a new "social cluster," but it is tempting to consider them a sign of the new times, provided we see the evolution of these labels as a conceptual reflection of new societal needs in urban communities and a niche for both innovative policymakers, planners, and analysts to address. Can it be that the social dimension reflected in the inclu-

sive city becomes more prominent aspect of the urban future than, say, economic or environmental ones, simply because current socio-economic situation in cities calls for it?

How Inclusive Can an Inclusive City Be?

The trend that cities, even those that have acquired fame as sustainable cities, smart cities, or knowledge cities, such as Amsterdam, Copenhagen, or Melbourne, also add the epithet inclusive to their name is unmistakable. Apparently, *inclusion* refers to a set of socially motivated ideals and related institutional actions that resonate well with social liberal sentiment appearing in the media, corporate community, political forums, and public debates in the Western world. The difficulty we encounter here is that the term "inclusive" often tends to be underdefined, that is, it is often left unsaid which social groups need to be included and what specific activities, opportunities, or spaces are under discussion. Or more precisely, which particular facilities, situations, or contexts need to be reorganized in order for a particular identified group of individuals to feel sufficiently included, and how this should be done without unduly violating the rights of others? When it comes to monetary capital and income, inclusion is primarily an economic issue and it is the financially underprivileged that are in need of support for full participation in the economic life of a thriving inclusive city. But if inclusion revolves around access to natural capital now and in the future, a broader ecological interpretation of inclusiveness comes to mind. Moreover, if it is religious, linguistic, gender, cultural, or age-related aspects that are under consideration, inclusion acquires socio-moral foundations, as for instance pushed in the cases of religious activism, radical feminism, anti-ageism groups, or the lesbian, gay, bisexual, transgender, queer, and intersex (LGBTQI) movement. Political inclusion may imply the involvement, consultation, or active participation of all these groups combined to ensure maximum representativeness of decision-making processes across large segments of society.

It seems obvious, at least at face value, that at a theoretical level any inclusive city would provide all of these groups based on all the above considerations and qualifications open access to its services and opportunities, but in practice things turn out not to be so simple. Including everybody in everything, all of the time and with same weight becomes a chimera as soon as there are conflicting interests and expectations and situations in which not all requests can be granted for justified reasons. For instance, as Richard Florida notes in both of his books mentioned above, the percentage of somehow "deviant social categories" tends to be higher among members of the creative class. In conservative societies, there tends to be little space for their ideas or open displays of their desires. And yet, they are economically far more successful than average. On the other hand, members of the working and service classes often feature more middle-of-the-road social and cultural preferences, but they are more weakly positioned in terms of employability and financial endowments. Accommodating the needs and wishes of both groups at all times is a complicated matter.

In the recent elections in many Western countries the propensity of working and service class—and to a degree also marginalized—voters to vote for nationalist and populist parties rose significantly, and this is beginning to challenge the ideals of more progressive and liberal segments of society. Realizing economic and social inclusion all at once is an attractive idea, but eventually necessitates a trading off among the various public values underlying these divergent views and interests expressed by their proponents (Bozeman, 2007). Disagreement and potential conflict are then inevitably the result of such cross-cutting political cleavages. A phenomenon that helps us to understand why inclusion may appear as locally contested issue is *nimbyism* (NIMBY is an acronym for "not in my back yard"). A safe middle-class neighborhood may find the flood of illegal immigrants or the establishment of a reception center for asylum seekers to the area disturbing and a significant decrease to their safety and quality of life. Whose rights and concerns should be addressed in the policymaking process and on what grounds? In multicultural societies, feminists may find the treatment of women in some religious communities deeply disturbing. In such cases, is the inclusion of male participants from ultraorthodox or orthodox Jewish, Christian, or Muslim communities that exclude female representatives from their own social group and resist or ignore arguments made by women from dominant white groups desirable? This boils down to the fact that inclusion is in effect a very challenging political issue. In addition, apart from previously discussed rights-based views, it is also worth considering how inclusion affects social order, safety, prosperity, and well-being of all segments of society, reminding us of a lasting ideological debate between liberalism and conservatism. In short, we need to be nuanced, sophisticated, and cautious when it comes to defining and legitimating the promotion of inclusion and assessing its long-term social and economic consequences.

Authors such as Hambleton (2015) place their bet on a progressive and optimistic conception of active democratic civic leadership composed of a broad alliance of governmental, societal, corporate, and other forces to realize the inclusive city. However much respect we have for his work and share his ideals regarding the achievement of inclusion in urban communities at various levels, we cannot deny that we fear not all is achievable at the same time in a democratic, open, and diverse society: different societal groups embrace different public values or at least do not prioritize them in the same ways. Realizing the inclusive city remains a hope, but what it eventually looks like and how it can be realized may well continue to depend on trade-offs among various conceptions and stakes represented in the inclusive city. Even though it appears that the label "inclusive city" will be consolidated alongside or on top of the creative, sustainable, and smart cities as an addition more attuned to the needs of the socio-economically polarized 2020s, it remains an issue, who actually will be included in what, on what grounds, and at what cost. We hope to throw more light on this issue in the following chapters of this book.

REFERENCES

Anttiroiko, A.-V. (2014). *The Political Economy of City Branding*. London and New York: Routledge.

Bozeman, B. (2007). *Public Values and Public Interest; Counterbalancing Economic Individualism*. Washington DC: Georgetown University Press.

Brynjolfsson, E., & McAfee, A. (2014). *The Second Machine age: Work, Progress, and Prosperity in a Time of Brilliant Technologies*. New York, NY: WW Norton & Company.

de Jong, M., Joss, S., Schraven, D., Zhan, C., & Weijnen, M. (2015). Sustainable–Smart–Resilient–Low Carbon–Eco–Knowledge Cities; Making Sense of a Multitude of Concepts Promoting Sustainable Urbanization. *Journal of Cleaner Production, 109,* 25–38.

Florida, R. (2002). *The Rise of the Creative Class: And How it's Transforming Work, Leisure, Community and Everyday Life*. New York: Perseus Book.

Florida, R. (2017). *The New Urban Crisis: How Our Cities are Increasing Inequality, Deepening Segregation, and Failing the Middle Class—and What We Can Do About It*. New York, NY: Basic Books.

Hambleton, R. (2015). *Leading the Inclusive City: Place-Based Innovation for a Bounded Planet*. Bristol, UK: Policy Press.

Joss, S. (2015). *Sustainable Cities; Governing for Urban Innovation*. London: Red Globe Press.

Ma, W., Schraven, D., de Bruijne, M., de Jong, M., & Lu, H. (2019). Tracing the Origins of Place Branding Research: A Bibliometric Study of Concepts in Use (1980–2018). *Sustainability, 11*(11). https://doi.org/10.3390/su11112999

Mayer, M. (2017). Whose city? From Ray Pahl's Critique of the Keynesian City to the Contestations Around Neoliberal Urbanism. *The Sociological Review, 65*(2), 168–183. https://doi.org/10.1111/1467-954X.12414

Pinson, G., & Morel Journel, C. (Eds.). (2017). *Debating the Neoliberal City.* London and New York: Routledge.

Schraven, D., Joss, S., & de Jong, M. (2020). Past, Present, Future: Engagement with Sustainable Urban Development Through 35 City Labels in the Research Literature 1990–2019. Manuscript submitted for publication.

Storper, M. (2016). The Neo-liberal City as Idea and Reality. *Territory, Politics, Governance, 4*(2), 241–263. https://doi.org/10.1080/2162267 1.2016.1158662

van Eijk, G. (2010). Exclusionary Policies are Not Just about the 'Neoliberal City': A Critique of Theories of Urban Revanchism and the Case of Rotterdam. *International Journal of Urban and Regional Research, 34*(4), 820–834. https://doi.org/10.1111/j.1468-2427.2010.00944.x

Conceptualizing Exclusion and Inclusion

Abstract The concepts "social inclusion" and "economic inclusion" can best be understood by examining the meaning and connotations of their opposite category, exclusion. Chapter 3 starts with outlining the reasons why people are historically excluded from various assets and services, which puts into a new light the widely cherished modern claim that social inclusion of groups and individuals is a moral "must." This moral duty seems to vary depending on the author and appears to have complex connections with the issues of social justice, equity, equality of outcome, equality of opportunity, social cohesion, and social capital. To estimate what shape realizing social and economic inclusion can or should take in cities, their prevailing values and norms need to be taken into account as well as the relevant institutional context. Different urban environments are likely to lead to different priorities and policy choices in creating inclusive cities.

Keywords Exclusion • Social Inclusion • Economic Inclusion • Equality of Outcome • Equality of Opportunity

INTRODUCTION

What does "inclusion" refer to in the context of urban development? In order to obtain a firm grasp of this concept, we will leave the urban dimension aside for a while and focus on the core meaning of inclusion as well as the broader conceptual field around it.

© The Author(s) 2020
A.-V. Anttiroiko, M. de Jong, *The Inclusive City*,
https://doi.org/10.1007/978-3-030-61365-5_3

The conceptual challenge we face in this regard is essentially socio-philosophical and ontological, since "inclusion" and "inclusive" direct our attention to a particular aspect of social reality, a kind of social in/out relay that determines social positions and relations individuals and groups have within a hierarchically structured society (Bourdieu, 1984; Espino, 2015). Such a discussion reveals how a pervasive role exclusion plays in determining social relations and how wealth, power, and social status are ideologically interwoven with the geography of work, housing, recreation, and mobility. It results in various forms of exploitation and oppression as well as in more subtle generally accepted acts of social control and exclusion (Allman, 2013; Sibley, 1995). This is the soil from which the idea of inclusion as a desirable goal for public policy emanated a few decades ago.

In this chapter, we will first make a brief excursion to the historical background of the terms "exclusion" and "inclusion." This is followed by an examination of related concepts in the wider conceptual field and the construal of a conceptual framework defining inclusion in two different dimensions: exclusion of whom (based on what criterion) as expressed in different types of social groups, and exclusion from what (space, position, opportunity) as expressed in different types of capital. Toward the end, we will turn our perspective around and shift from the "personal pain and injustice" of not being socially included in consuming something considered valuable by a particular person to the wider societal "gain and benefit" of being economically included in value generation. In other words, we focus on how the morality of social inclusion may justify and be advanced by economic inclusion.

From Exclusion to Inclusion

Modern-day political and academic discussions about "inclusion" can, in our view, best be understood through its antonym, *exclusion*. To comprehend the nature of these concepts, we should adopt an evolutionary point of view. Exclusion and inclusion can be seen as natural features of social life, which emerged as an inherent part of the historical evolution of human societies. Their basic function is to create a demarcation between "us" and "them" and this has been essential in managing social interaction, creating hierarchies, determining and defending borders, organizing community life, and protecting immediate private, group, or communal interests (Allman, 2013).

Practically all traditional and even modern institutions and arrangements serve some exclusionary functions as they draw demarcations between in-group and out-group, between privileged and underprivileged. Kinship, marriage, and citizenship, for example, all include and exclude people in one way or another (e.g., Jackson, 1999; Rawal, 2008). For this reason, it is to a certain extent natural that in a modern society we are affected by rules and regulations that occasionally set strict conditions for including us in or denying our access to participation in or control over certain social spaces, systems, or functions. This implies that all of us can claim to be excluded from many things in a number of ways even when operating in open, democratic, and egalitarian societies (Estivill, 2003).

Social inclusion is a child of modernity. That is, the critical stance toward exclusion and the moral imperative to promote social inclusion emanated from the pores of the intersection of capitalism, industrialization, and democratization. The nineteenth century was, most notably in Europe, an age of ideologies that coincided with nationalistic tendencies which had strengthened after the rise of the nation-states and culminated in the great upheavals through Europe around 1848, known as the Spring of Nations. It fed national identities and supported nation-building processes, thus generating inclusionary and exclusionary tendencies at the same time. Some of the aims of these processes included demands for more citizen participation, greater freedom of the press, and claims that the conditions of the working class needed drastic improvement. Important steps taken in realizing these large-scale inclusionary policies included a modern conception of labor rights, national social insurance schemes, and women's universal suffrage and their right to stand for elections.

The twentieth century witnessed a rapidly changing ideological scene with a considerable weakening of conservative ethnocentrism. After World War II it had degenerated to become an underdog facing growing pressure from radical countercultures, social movements, and the emergence of the welfare state. Especially following the rise of political movements promoting the acceptance of various identities, activist groups began to view society through the lens of structural oppression and collective victimhood. A left-leaning cultural semi-revolution evoked a persuasive identity struggle reminiscent of the century-old Marxist idea of class struggle, which legitimized attacks against modern institutions, authorities, and belief systems (Anttiroiko, 2019). It emerged arguably as the most influential agenda-setter on inclusion on both sides of the Atlantic, paying special attention to marginalized people's ability to participate effectively in economic, social, political, and cultural life, which thus stretched the meaning of exclusion toward any kind of alienation and distance from mainstream society (Duffy, 1995). This development was instrumental in the gradual mainstreaming of inclusionary policies, with gender equality and emancipation of various types of minorities coming to mind as primary instances.

Western democracies began to address social and economic exclusion on a larger scale during the 1980s and 1990s (e.g., Levitas, 2005; Lister, 1998). This move gained significant ideological and operational support from international organizations, such as the OECD, the IMF and the World Bank, and regional organizations, the most influential among them being the European Union (Rawal, 2008; Sen, 2000). In short, striving for a transition toward an egalitarian and inclusive society became the prevailing trend throughout the Western world, which was instrumental in the global mainstreaming of the idea of an inclusive society (Estivill, 2003).

UNDERSTANDING SOCIAL EXCLUSION

The modern concept of exclusion finds its historical precedent in views on poverty (Estivill, 2003, p. 9). The distinction between poverty and social exclusion was placed on the public and political agendas in the 1970s. One of the milestones was René Lenoir's *Les exclus: un Français sur dix* published in 1974. It pictured the life of the disabled, single parents, uninsured unemployed, and other disadvantaged groups who were excluded from participation in a wide range of social and economic activities and whose deprivation caused a deeply and painfully felt lack of opportunity in improving their quality of life (Hayes, Gray, & Edwards, 2008; Estivill, 2003, p. 5). Another landmark study worth mentioning is Peter Townsend's *Poverty in the United Kingdom*, published in 1979, which addressed the connection between poverty and social exclusion. He argued that there was a level of income below which people were unable to participate in normal life in society (Levitas, 1996).

In the following decades, various scholars—Room (1995), Atkinson (1998), Bynner (1999), and Sen (2000)—began to see the concept of poverty as inadequate against the various types of disadvantages experienced by marginalized individuals and groups in modern society. For example, social exclusion due to physical disability does not necessarily involve poverty. The same goes for many other forms of exclusion. At the individual level, exclusion is rather about breakdown in relationships with immediate family, community, or wider society. That said, material poverty remains a relevant category, for it certainly tends to narrow people's perspectives and chances to experience success and a rich range of social experiences. It may lead to deprivation and unfavorable outcomes in terms of quality of life and the exertion and fulfillment of civil, political, and social rights (Bynner, 1999; Room, 1995).

When considering the development of an inclusive city, understanding the causes and consequences of exclusion is of vital importance. Defining aspects include the relativity, agency, and dynamics of exclusion (Atkinson, 1998). Exclusion is conceptually challenging due to its multidimensional, relational, processual, and context-specific nature (see e.g. Burchardt et al., 2002). An anthropological perspective helps us come to terms with the drivers, forms, and outcomes of social exclusion through spotting agency and social relations in their structural and cultural contexts. It is essentially a matter of observing people's everyday lives as members of their communities and societies over a long period of time. For the privileged, this implies a wish to distinguish themselves from others deemed "lower" by displaying various physical tokens of distinction in wear, behavioral mode, or presence in and control of places and spaces for dwelling, working, recreation, and transport. For the underprivileged, there would rather be a lack of access to or participation in opportunities and activities and lower levels of expectation for chances of success and enjoyment in life and future prospects to change the status quo (Bynner, 1999; Davey & Gordon, 2017; Espino, 2015; Sen, 2000). Silver (2007) describes social exclusion aptly as:

[a] multidimensional process of progressive social rupture, detaching groups and individuals from social relations and institutions and preventing them from full participation in the normal, normatively prescribed activities of the society in which they live. (p. 15)

Even if exclusion is seen primarily as a negative position and starting point for building relations in human societies, Estivill (2003, p. 15) reminds us of the importance to avoid sketching too idyllic a picture of a harmonious and cohesive society, as it may detach us from the reality in which exclusion in many occasions serves legitimate functions.

CONCRETE FORMS OF EXCLUSION

Developing a comprehensive and definitive conceptualization of social inclusion is not only an exceptionally demanding task but would also be less useful for our purposes. Namely, we need to clarify its essential features in terms of its most evident forms in the urban context and extend discussion toward economic dimension of exclusion and inclusion. For this purpose, we will build a matrix that demonstrates the most typical relational aspects of social inclusion, that is, on what grounds certain groups are excluded from something, and what are the things they exactly excluded from? Thus, in a rather pragmatic fashion, we may identify two primary dimensions of the dialectic relation that determines the degree of exclusion and inclusion:

(1) The first dimension lists all grounds or criteria on the basis of which individuals or groups in society are excluded from or included in something. These can be any features of their being or identity, which are considered legitimate reasons for not being entitled to one or more types and forms of prosperity. We identified age, physical and mental (dis)ability, religion and ideology, race and ethnicity, gender and sexual orientation, level of income or wealth, and geographical location (nationality, residence, or otherwise) as examples of possible grounds for ex-/inclusion.

(2) The second dimension offers five types of capital individuals or groups that are excluded from or included in to obtain access to aspects of prosperity deemed valuable. Since in principle, assets can represent anything of value, we approached them through the angle of entitlements people have to different types of capital: human and cultural capital (knowledge, education, skills, culture), social capital (precious personal and professional networks), financial capital (any sort of public or private source of wealth or income expressed in monetary terms), physical capital (objects in the built environment such as infrastructures, real estate, or mobile objects), and natural capital (any planetary resource naturally present in the environment, such as fresh air, land, water, and resources located inside them).

These two dimensions are illustrated in Fig. 3.1. Note that the fact that we operationalized valuable entitlements as various forms of capital implies that civil and political rights are taken for granted in this scheme. Explicit discussion about political capital is omitted due to our focus on social and economic ex-/inclusion in the urban context.

Figure 3.1 illustrates that exclusionary societies exert strong forms of religious or political discrimination excluding minorities from access to many forms of human capital (universities or drama performances), social capital (membership in various organizations or communities relevant to career-making or participation in professional meetings), financial capital (eligibility to tax discounts or relevant subsidy schemes), physical capital (using public transport or access to buildings), or natural capital (admission to parks, or availability of fresh air and water); these may be paired

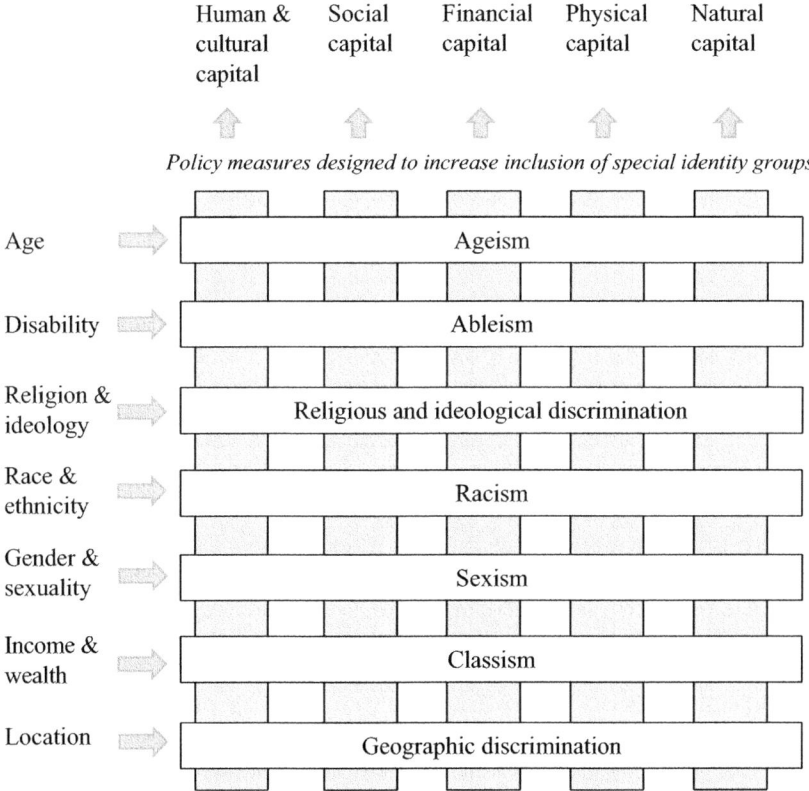

Fig. 3.1 The matrix of the forms of exclusion and the types of capital

with limitations in civil and legal rights (suffrage or equal access to recourse before courts). Less egregious examples of exclusion well-known in some democratic societies include employers' negative attitudes toward older workers; the difficulty of ethnic minorities to realize their potential in higher education; limited or no access for lower-income groups to affordable housing; and the exclusion women may experience in obtaining valuable social capital amidst "old boys' networks" or the fact that having children often comes at a significant cost for women's earnings and careers.

SOCIAL EXCLUSION AND INCLUSION IN CONTEXT

Social exclusion and inclusion, due to their multidimensionality and relationality, always ought to be understood in context. This becomes apparent when one imagines how the ideals, institutional arrangements, and practical instances of social inclusion vary from one nation to another and between regions or specific locations within a country. Each community has its own history, culture, and regulatory structures, which all affect different dimensions of social exclusion and their interplay as well as institutional measures designed to deal with them. Such contexts matter primarily as they constitute a mix of exclusionary and inclusionary arrangements, which jointly determine our access to resources and life-chances (Silver, 2015).

Regarding societal context, as progressive or interventionist types of institutional environments there are solidaristic and egalitarian welfare states with high levels of taxation, comprehensive support systems, and active governments, as seen in the Nordic countries. A paradigmatic case of a socially stratified state capitalist or patrimonial system where a much larger share of the opportunities and resources are allocated to the ruling class has its manifestations in many Latin American and African countries. A third type is that of the Anglo-Saxon style capitalist system where equality of opportunity replaces equality of outcomes and where government action is far more restrained than, say, in Northern Europe. Actual specific contexts in countries, regions, and communities are undoubtedly much more nuanced and detailed than sketched above, but these three ideal-types present a first approximation of how contextual differences relevant to aspects of inclusion and exclusion can be approached at the outset.

There is no absolute yardstick according to which one can offer indications or demarcations to determine or preemptively justify who should be excluded from or included in something. In other words, there is no single center of social integration or sole criterion for establishing who should be "in" and "out," or even who is privileged to be in some position or receive something and who is excluded from such entitlements or resources (Jackson, 1999; Rawal, 2008). Moreover, these rules may apply differently to different spheres of life. For example, we could well imagine a society where people who are privileged in terms of wealth are still excluded from certain positions or spaces revolving around cultural capabilities or academic knowledge and thus be excluded from environments of which they may well aspire in vain to join the ranks. To generalize, in pluralistic societies where wealth, power, and social status do not coincide, various forms of non-overlapping or intersecting exclusion will appear. Moreover, even in strongly stratified societies, privileged strata or classes will not be fully homogenous: there will always be grounds for excluding certain people from certain positions or spaces. Relying on fixed group identities and a fixed hierarchy of categorical disadvantages is problematic when considering the issues of exclusion and inclusion: the specific context in which phenomena appear invariably needs to be taken into account to form a sound judgment.

A final remark to be made here regarding the contextualization of social inclusion is the fact that not all forms and versions of inclusion can be realized synchronically. Often, as in the case of policy priorities or the fulfillment of various public values, anticipated and unanticipated side-effects appear where the consequences of measures aimed at promoting one form of inclusion will affect the level of other forms. One of the most fundamental trade-offs concerning social and economic inclusion is whether generous welfare state systems realizing social equality of outcome cause a significant decrease in the potential to generate equality of opportunity (e.g., Headey, Goodin, Muffels, & Dirven, 2000). Another family of social inclusion trade-offs relates to identity politics, the paradigmatic case being the application of affirmative action. Such measures may lead to higher levels of inclusion of disadvantaged groups in the short term, but if their performance or appearance is seen as of inferior quality, this may undermine long-term confidence in the capabilities of the members of that underprivileged identity group. In addition, it may fuel tensions between different groups and even within groups. In general, favoring some gender, age group, ethnicity, or any other group in society—and thus improving their social and/or economic inclusion as a group—may occasionally imply that less resources are allocated to other target groups or that some others are required to pay higher contributions to finance extra costs caused by improved inclusion. In short, the multidimensionality and contextuality of social inclusion make the appearance of unexpected effects of measures taken and the need to weigh the importance of certain types of inclusion over others more than likely. Social exclusion and inclusion are thus extremely subtle and multifaceted phenomena, which involve complex policy challenges that resemble those of multi-objective optimization.

SOCIAL INCLUSION AND RELATED CONCEPTS

Even if exclusion and inclusion are in fact different sides of the same coin, the shift in emphasis from the former to the latter has important implications for the way the central policy challenge is addressed. While studying social exclusion primarily identifies the normality of different individuals or occupying certain positions or spaces, taking the angle of promoting social inclusion rather problematizes the fact that not all people enjoy such privileges and enjoin planners and policymakers with the moral challenge to effectively enable them to reach these positions and spaces. Social inclusion has turned things into a constructive and development-oriented assignment (cf. Silver, 2015). Below, we examine the concept of social inclusion more in-depth and explore the broader conceptual field around it.

The World Bank (n.d.) has defined social inclusion both in generic terms as conditions that are conducive to people's ability as members of society to take part in it, and in specific terms as actions associated with the eradication of poverty and improving the conditions of disadvantaged groups. Hilary Silver (2015) describes the two sides of social inclusion as (a) a process encouraging social interaction between people, and as (b) an impersonal institutional mechanism of opening up access to participation in all spheres of social life. According to her, social inclusion is

> a multi-dimensional, relational process of increasing opportunities for social participation, enhancing capabilities to fulfill normatively prescribed social roles, broadening social ties of respect and recognition, and at the collective level, enhancing social bonds, cohesion, integration, or solidarity. (pp. 2–3)

There are several widely used concepts which have family resemblance with social inclusion as well as concepts that can be used to define some aspects of social inclusion. Some of those related concepts belong to the family of moral justification with four major categories. First, (i) concepts such as social justice, equity, and equality of outcome describe morally motivated objectives or end results, while (ii) concepts like equality of opportunity, solidarity, and fairness are primarily relational, describing conditions or intentions that are conducive to socially acceptable end results. The other (iii) set of related concepts is based on utility, benefit, or desirability. Accordingly, some concepts describe the result or outcome, in the same way as social justice, but with a less pronounced ethical focus. These include concepts such as social cohesion, harmony, happiness, and wellbeing. Lastly, the fourth major (iv) conceptual category describes socially beneficial conditions, in the same way as equality of opportunity, but with a weaker connection to moral judgment and stronger connection with preconditions, capacities, or procedures, as with social capital and sharing.

We may say that social inclusion is philosophically grounded in social justice. It is rooted in religious doctrines of helping less fortunate people, those who are weak, sick, or oppressed, and it has since become an important element in various ideologies which hold that all citizens should be treated equally (Ornstein, 2017; see also Rawls, 1985). The label "social" places the consideration of justice into a broadly defined societal context, referring in practical terms to issues of wealth or status, which determine an individual's standing in society. The social dimension makes realizing justice a conceptually challenging task, since this extends the scope of the concept to all socially relevant outcomes generated by the system. All reasons why inequalities exist are then associated with social structures and effectively detached from individual choices and responsibilities (Whaples, 2019). Social justice is about how justly the level of wealth and privileges people have is distributed in a given society. Hence, the step to equity is not a large one to take. Equity is often equated with equality of outcome, which implies that everyone's capabilities and assets are equalized to such a degree so that everyone should have the potential to reach the same level of satisfaction. Equity gives everyone a taste of success by leveling the ground in the micro-context at hand and is thus aimed at equalizing life-chances within a community through corrective arrangements (On equity in development, see Jones, 2009). Achieving equality of outcome requires large-scale state intervention.

The second concept referring to a moral condition is equality and, more precisely, equality of opportunity. This condition is sometimes described as social solidarity or an expression of altruism, built upon an idea of selfless consideration and contribution to the welfare of others (e.g., Oosterlynck, Schuermans, & Loopmans, 2017). Realizing equality of opportunity requires creating conditions for a level playing field seen as fair to all people involved, which rests on appropriate institutional arrangements (Rawls, 1985). Equality means that everyone is provided similar starting conditions and procedurally treated in the same manner. This implies the absence of factors or obstacles that discriminate against any actor and describes the state of being equal, especially in status, rights, or opportunities. It is not necessarily about seeing actors identical or similar per se, but rather, in a prescriptive sense, assuming that they are equivalent or have the same "relational weight" or operational conditions in a given social, political, or economic context (cf. Gosepath, 2011).

Probably the most important conceptual distinction in current philosophical discussions is that between two different views of equality: equality of outcome (as under the conceptual category i), and equality of opportunity (as under the conceptual category ii). The latter refers to the fair conditions and rules according to which everyone is allowed to pursue their aims, while the former hints at the conditions creating similar or even the same end results in a given domain for all members of society (Gosepath, 2011). Since the financial affordability of keeping a welfare state and society in place has come under threat in many parts of the world since the 1980s and 1990s, many governments shifted their focus from policies based on social rights and equality of outcome as philosophical foundation toward one of social inclusion and equality of opportunity (e.g., Lister, 1998).

The relevant third family of concepts to be discussed here is that of the socially desirable end results as defined in more utilitarian terms, crystallized in the concept of social cohesion. This strand of ideas is connected with such concepts as well-being, welfare, quality of life, and happiness. Although utility-based views of policymaking are certainly imbued with particular moral assumptions, the imperative for governments to act may be less heavy-handed and more narrowly economic rather than broadly social in nature. As in the previous cases, the sets of definitions for social cohesion in the literature show a fragmented picture. The most pertinent discussions in this regard relate to general societal well-being and proportional representation of various groups in society. Such definitions show commonalities such as the well-being of all members of the group, alongside shared values such as trust and harmony in society (Fonseca, Lukosch, & Brazier, 2019; Fukuyama, 1996). Prior research has identified several relevant factors that play a role in social cohesion, which consistently point out the need for a balanced society with equal opportunities and rights for all citizens. A cohesive society works toward the well-being of all its members, creates a sense of belonging, and targets the prevention of marginalization within and between different groups (OECD, 2011).

The fourth and last set of family-resembling concepts includes social capital and sharing, which can be characterized as beneficial conditions for social action and organization. The presence of social capital can act as a major contributor to social inclusiveness. The contention then is that social relationships, networks, and trustful relations are resources that can lead to favorable outcomes in social life or, in general, enable society to function effectively under given conditions (for definitions of social capital, see, e.g., Sato, 2013). In its current use, there are a few classic works that are particularly influential, one being the seminal work by Robert Putnam (1993). He understood social capital as a community-level resource and defined it as networks, norms, and social trust that facilitate coordination and cooperation for mutual benefit. A related concept, sharing, as a colloquial term refers to giving a portion of something to or using something jointly with other people. Currently, it is popular under the umbrella of the sharing economy, which describes the joint use of resources or, more precisely, peer-to-peer-based activity of acquiring, providing, or sharing access to goods and services, usually facilitated by a digital platform (see McLaren & Agyeman, 2015). On the other hand, there are alternative views according to which sharing represents a new economic model aimed at rebuilding social ties claimed to have been lost due to the pervasive influence of an alienating market culture (see Parsons, 2014). Realizing such beneficial but intangible amenities as social capital or trust cannot possibly be realized by active enforcement but rather through gentle encouragement by governments in coordination with other relevant stakeholders.

Refocusing on Economic Inclusion

Thus far, when referring to exclusion and inclusion, we have primarily referred to it in the context of "the social." In essence, however, inclusion is a broad denominator of societal and/or interpersonal relations, which could refer to a great variety of aspects, such as legal, political, financial, cultural, spatial, and environmental ones. Even temporal inclusion could be distinguished to the extent that environmental or other aspects of inclusion do not cover the interests of future generations.

In this book, we wish to highlight the importance of economic inclusion, which relates to poverty reduction, greater income equality, and employment opportunities (Silver, 2015). The reason for doing this is essentially that we plead for a shift in perspective away from focusing on claiming and forcing off social inclusion, which evokes defensive reactions on the part of those required to relinquish their grasp over desired forms of capital, to viewing the situation as making use of different types of capital that various individuals and groups have at their disposal. Such a shift draws attention away from problems and what is missing to opportunities and why and how various individuals and groups are necessary for value creation. Missing the chance to input the human, social, physical, or natural capital people have leads to missed opportunities, waste of resources, and eventually an aggregate welfare loss. In other words, turning the logic around releases positive rather than negative energy, which is helpful for societal problem-solving and the creation of prosperity in a broad sense of the word.

The shift in perspective is doubly important in light of today's winner-takes-all trend in capital accumulation. Economic growth is not only narrowly defined, but there is also an alarming trend that seemingly positive development revealed in GDP is increasingly "exclusive" in terms of how the fruits of economic growth are shared between different segments of society (Florida, 2017; Mayer, 2018; Piiparinen, 2019). At the global level, this is seen in the extreme concentration of wealth, with roughly 1% of the world population controlling almost half of the world's wealth. This is a phenomenon that has its expression in urban development as well, for paradoxically inequality seems to have reached its peak in the most successful cities (Florida, 2017; Kotkin, 2014). In addition, the "great decoupling" appears as a critical dividing factor associated with the new economy, in which GDP gains have become disconnected from the growth of employment and household income (Brynjolfsson & McAfee, 2014). Moreover, value extraction consistently trumps value creation in an economy increasingly affected by digitization, platformization, and financialization, which in combination give exponentially more power to speculative elements in capitalist economies (Mazzucato, 2018). In an economic environment plagued by extreme income disparities and wealth concentration, it has become imperative to pay more attention not only to various forms of social inclusion, but also to a vastly more inclusive conception of capital: the one that goes way beyond a monetary or financial interpretation alone, and the one that conceives how large segments of society need each other as stakeholders in a joint enterprise toward inclusive urban prosperity.

There is ample empirical evidence supporting the claim that economic inclusion is good for growth and vice versa (Mayer, 2018; Roche & Jakub, 2017; Shafique et al., 2019). *Inclusive growth* is a process that encourages long-run growth by improving the productivity of individuals and firms in order to raise sustainable living standards for all (Managi, 2019; Parilla, 2017). This implies a paradigm shift in local economic development policy and in the work of economic development agencies (Donahue, McDearman, & Barker, 2017). The economic end of this idea can be referred to as *economic inclusion*, covering such themes as inclusive workplaces, inclusive business that benefits low-income communities, and inclusive business that adopt a corporate culture that values tolerance, diversity, multiculturalism, and social inclusion and on that basis improves its engagement with employees, customers, and other stakeholders (Donovan & Kaplan, 2019; Wiley-Little, 2013; Porter & Kramer, 2011). Such an approach has its rationale in inclusive growth and in the reflections of diversity, tolerance, and political correctness in business, sometimes referred to as *economic correctness*, an economic counterpart of political correctness.

Besides this, the inclusive city maximizes the utilization of *entrepreneurial potential* of the urban community and harvests the pool of capacities local people, groups, and institutions can provide. A step toward such a "social" direction is referred to as *social economy*, which consists of a family of solidaristic, social, and community-oriented enterprises and organizations—cooperatives, mutuals, associations, foundations, and social enterprises—that share the view of the primacy of solidarism and social objectives over market logic and capital accumulation.

Economic life and inclusion also meet at the level of empowered *individuals and groups* with their opportunities, choices, loyalties, and responsibilities. This view emphasizes people's efforts in creating value in their own local communities and showing their commitment to the utilization of the types of capital they own and control for their own benefit as well as that of community around them (Gibson-Graham & the Community Economies Collective, 2017).

Our view of the *inclusive city* is built upon a notion of inclusion with value creation and sharing in mind. It is a city with inclusive structures and processes that generate and share prosperity to be enjoyed by various segments of society, including those that are usually left out of such considerations. To sum up, in the context of local economic development, the concept of *inclusive city* refers to an urban community in which (a) business as usual takes a positive stance toward inclusion and diversity, (b) inclusion is used to harness local entrepreneurial and innovative potential,

(c) social innovators and entrepreneurs constitute an essential part of the economy, and (d) members of the community are both invited and expected to utilize their innovative and value-generating potential for both their private benefit (defined in a broad sense of the word with various forms of capital incorporated) and that of the entire community they are part of.

Toward Shared Prosperity

The material side of the inclusive city boils down to the idea of inclusive or shared prosperity. Globally, the most important advocates of inclusive prosperity are international organizations, such as the World Bank and the OECD. Inclusion is actually an in-built element of the rationale behind the World Bank Group, which strives for two goals: to end extreme poverty globally and to boost shared prosperity in every country. The latter, *shared prosperity*, is of vital importance here. The World Bank describes this goal as follows:

> Promoting shared prosperity means that we will work to increase the incomes and welfare of the poorer segments of society wherever they are, be it the poorest of nations or thriving middle- or high-income countries. This indicator departs from the traditional focus on growth of the average income of the population—an approach that implicitly assumes that economic growth automatically trickles down to the poor. (World Bank, 2019)

While economic growth has lifted millions out of poverty, the other side of the coin is growing inequality. Polarization implies that most countries have experienced difficulties in sustaining economic growth and social stability over time. It looks obvious that without a significant reduction in inequality the world will not meet the ambitious global development goals agreed at the UN in 2015 to end extreme poverty by 2030. One of the major concerns is the observation that in far too many places a rising share of revenues is taken in by a tiny fraction of earners. Here we touch on a key policy issue: this rise in inequality is not an inevitable consequence of economic growth as such. There are various ways to balance allocation and distribution. In fact, we need to pay attention to issues of social justice exactly because of our pursuit of long-term growth and social stability. In the inclusive city, promoting broad economic participation is expected to enhance the translation of economic growth into poverty reduction and better opportunities for broad segments of society (World Bank, 2019).

REFERENCES

Allman, D. (2013, January-March). The Sociology of Social Inclusion. *SAGE Open*, 1–16.

Anttiroiko, A.-V. (2019). Paradoxes of Identity Politics and Gender Mainstreaming: The Case of Nordic Countries. *International Journal of Policy Studies, 10*(1), 151–160.

Atkinson, A. (1998). Social Exclusion, Poverty and Unemployment. In A. Atkinson & J. Hills (Eds.), *Exclusion Employment and Opportunity* (CASE Paper No. 4). London: Centre for the Analysis of Social Exclusion, London School of Economics (LSE).

Bourdieu, P. (1984). *Distinction; A Social Critique of the Judgement of Taste*. Cambridge MA: Harvard University Press.

Brynjolfsson, E., & McAfee, A. (2014). *The Second Machine age: Work, Progress, and Prosperity in a Time of Brilliant Technologies*. New York, NY: WW Norton & Company.

Burchardt, T., Le Grand, J., & Piachaud, D. (2002). Degrees of Exclusion: Developing a Dynamic, Multidimensional Measure. In J. Hills, J. Le Grand, & D. Piachaud (Eds.), *Understanding Social Exclusion*. Oxford: Oxford University Press.

Bynner, J. (1999). *Risks and Outcomes of Social Exclusion Insights from Longitudinal Data*. Paris: OECD.

Davey, S., & Gordon, S. (2017). Definitions of Social Inclusion and Social Exclusion: The Invisibility of Mental Illness and the Social Conditions of Participation. *International Journal of Culture and Mental Health, 10*(3), 229–237. https://doi.org/10.1080/17542863.2017.1295091

Donahue, R., McDearman, B., & Barker, R. (2017). Committing To Inclusive Growth: Lessons for metro areas from the Inclusive Economic Development Lab. Metropolitan Policy Program. Washington, D.C.: Brookings. Retrieved November 12, 2019, from https://www.brookings.edu/wp-content/uploads/2017/09/metro_20170927_committing-to-inclusive-growth-iedl-report.pdf

Donovan, M., & Kaplan, M. (2019). *The Inclusion Dividend: Why Investing in Diversity & Inclusion Pays Off*. DG Press.

Duffy, K. (1995). *Social Exclusion and Human Dignity in Europe: Background Report for the Proposed Initiative by the Council of Europe*. Strasbourg: Council of Europe.

Espino, N. A. (2015). *Building the Inclusive City; Theory and Practice for Confronting Urban Segregation*. London: Routledge.

Estivill, J. (2003). *Concepts and Strategies for Combatting Social Exclusion: An Overview*. Geneva: International Labor Office—STEP/Portugal.

Florida, R. (2017). *The New Urban Crisis: How Our Cities are Increasing Inequality, Deepening Segregation, and Failing the Middle Class—And What We Can Do About It*. New York, NY: Basic Books.

Fonseca, X., Lukosch, S., & Brazier, F. (2019). Social Cohesion Revisited: A New Definition and How to Characterize it. *Innovation: The European Journal of Social Science Research, 32*(2), 231–253. https://doi.org/10.1080/1351161 0.2018.1497480

Fukuyama, F. (1996). *Trust; The Social Virtues and the Creation of Prosperity*. New York: The Free Press.

Gibson-Graham, J. K., & the Community Economies Collective. (2017). *Cultivating Community Economies: Tools for Building a Liveable World*. Retrieved October 23, 2020, from https://thenextsystem.org/sites/default/files/2017-08/JKGibsonGraham-1-1.pdf

Gosepath, S. (2011). Equality. In Edward N. Zalta (Ed.), *The Stanford Encyclopedia of Philosophy* (Spring 2011 Edition). Retrieved October 23, 2020, from https://plato.stanford.edu/archives/spr2011/entries/equality/

Hayes, A., Gray, M., & Edwards, B. (2008). Social Inclusion: Origins, Concepts and Key Themes. Australian Government. Social Inclusion Unit, Canberra. Retrieved October 4, 2019, from http://pandora.nla.gov.au/pan/142909/20130920-1300/www.socialinclusion.gov.au/sites/default/files/publications/pdf/si-origins-concepts-themes.pdf.

Headey, B., Goodin, R. E., Muffels, R., & Dirven, H.-J. (2000). Is There a Trade-Off between Economic Efficiency and a Generous Welfare State? A Comparison of Best Cases of 'The Three Worlds of Welfare Capitalism. *Social Indicators Research, 50*(2), 115–157.

Jackson, C. (1999). Social Exclusion and Gender: Does One Size Fit All? *The European Journal of Development Research, 11*(1), 125–146.

Jones, H. (2009). *Equity in Development: Why it Is Important and How to Achieve It*. Working Paper 311. London: Overseas Development Institute. Retrieved December 8, 2019, from https://www.odi.org/sites/odi.org.uk/files/odi-assets/publications-opinion-files/4577.pdf

Kotkin, J. (2014). *The New Class Conflict*. Dagenham: Central Books.

Lenoir, R. (1974). *Les exclus: un Français sur dix*. Paris: Seuil.

Levitas, R. (1996). The Concept of Social Exclusion and the New Durkheimian Hegemony. *Critical Social Policy, 16*(46), 5–20.

Levitas, R. (2005). *The Inclusive Society?: Social Exclusion and New Labour*. London: Palgrave Macmillan.

Lister, R. (1998). From Equality to Social Inclusion: New Labour and the Welfare State. *Critical Social Policy, 18*(55), 215–225. https://doi.org/10.1177/026101839801805505

Managi, S. (Ed.). (2019). *Wealth, Inclusive Growth ad Sustainability.* London: Routledge.

Mayer, C. (2018). *Prosperity: Better Business Makes the Greater Good.* Oxford: Oxford University Press.

Mazzucato, M. (2018). *The Value of Everything: Making and Taking in the Global Economy.* London: Allen Lane.

McLaren, D., & Agyeman, J. (2015). *Sharing Cities: A Case for Truly Smart and Sustainable Cities.* Cambridge, MA: MIT Press.

OECD. (2011). *Perspectives on Global Development 2012: Social Cohesion in a Shifting World.* Paris: OECD. https://doi.org/10.1787/persp_glob_dev-2012-en

Oosterlynck, S., Schuermans, N., & Loopmans, M. (Eds.). (2017). *Place, Diversity and Solidarity* (1st ed.). London: Routledge.

Ornstein, A. C. (2017). Social Justice: History, Purpose and Meaning. *Society, 54*(6), 541–548.

Parilla, J. (2017). Opportunity for Growth: How Reducing Barriers to Economic Inclusion can Benefit Workers, Firms, and Local Economies. Metropolitan Policy Program. Washington, D.C.: Brookings. Retrieved November 12, 2019, from https://www.brookings.edu/wp-content/uploads/2017/09/metro_20170927_opportunity-for-growth-iedl-report-parilla-final.pdf

Parsons, A. (2014, March 5). The Sharing Economy: A Short Introduction to its Political Evolution. *Opendemocracy.* Retrieved October 18, 2019, from https://www.opendemocracy.net/en/transformation/sharing-economy-short-introduction-to-its-political-evolution/

Piiparinen, R. (2019, October 4). The Inclusive Growth Problem. *CityLab.* Retrieved November 12, 2019, from https://www.citylab.com/perspective/2019/10/inclusive-growth-economic-disparities-rust-belt-inequality/599347/

Porter, M. E., & Kramer, M. R. (2011, January-February). Creating Shared Value: How to Reinvent Capitalism—and Unleash a Wave of Innovation and Growth. *Harvard Business Review, 89*(1–2), 62–77.

Putnam, R. (1993). *Making Democracy Work: Civic Traditions in Modern Italy.* Princeton, NJ: Princeton University Press.

Rawal, N. (2008). Social Inclusion and Exclusion: A Review. *Dhaulagiri Journal of Sociology and Anthropology, 2,* 161–180. Retrieved from https://www.cmi.no/file/?589

Rawls, J. (1985). Justice as Fairness: Political not Metaphysical. *Philosophy and Public Affairs, 14*(3), 223–251.

Roche, B., & Jakub, J. (2017). *Completing Capitalism: Heal Business to Heal the World*. Oakland, CA: Berrett Koehler Publishers.

Room, G. (Ed.). (1995). *Beyond the Threshold: The Measurement and Analysis of Social Exclusion*. Bristol, UK: University of Bristol. The Policy Press.

Sato, Y. (2013). Social Capital. In: Sociopedia.isa. Retrieved October 17, 2019, from http://www.sagepub.net/isa/resources/pdf/SocialCapital.pdf

Sen, A. (2000). Social Exclusion: Concept, Application, and Scrutiny. Social Development Papers No. 1. Manila: Asian Development Bank. Retrieved October 10, 2019, from https://www.adb.org/sites/default/files/publication/29778/social-exclusion.pdf

Shafique, A., Antink, B., Clay, A., & Cox, E. (2019). Inclusive Growth in Action: Snapshots of a New Economy. London: Royal Society for the Encouragement of Arts, Manufactures and Commerce (RSA). Retrieved December 7, 2019, from https://www.thersa.org/globalassets/pdfs/reports/rsa-inclusive-growth-in-action.pdf

Sibley, D. (1995). *Geographies of Exclusion: Society and Difference in the West*. London: Routledge.

Silver, H. (2007, September). *Social Exclusion: Comparative Analysis of Europe and Middle East Youth*. Wolfensohn Center for Development & Dubai School of Government. Middle East Youth Initiative Working Paper, Number 1. Retrieved October 19, 2019, from https://www.meyi.org/uploads/3/2/0/1/32012989/silver_-_social_exclusion-comparative_analysis_of_europe_and_middle_east_youth.pdf

Silver, H. (2015). *The Contexts of Social Inclusion*. DESA Working Paper No. 144. ST/ESA/2015/DWP/144, October 2015. Department of Economic and Social Affairs. New York: United Nations.

Townsend, P. (1979). *Poverty in the United Kingdom*. London: Allen Lane and Penguin Books.

Whaples, R. M. (2019). New Thinking about Social Justice. *The Independent Review, 24*(1), 5–11.

Wiley-Little, A. D. (2013). *Profitable Diversity: How Economic Inclusion Can Lead to Success*. Minneapolis, MN: Two Harbors Press.

World Bank. (2019, October 2). Inequality and Shared Prosperity: Overview. Retrieved October 16, 2019, from https://www.worldbank.org/en/topic/isp/overview

World Bank. (n.d.). Social Inclusion. Retrieved October 24, 2019, from https://www.worldbank.org/en/topic/social-inclusion

CHAPTER 4

Dimensions of Exclusion

Abstract In order to operationalize economic inclusion in cities, Chap. 4 describes four aspects in exclusion that need to be mapped in specific circumstances. First, exclusion ground—for example, age, ability, religion, race, gender, income, and location—indicates the explicit or implicit criterion for exclusion. Second, types of capital, including human, social, financial, physical, and natural capital, depict the access to types of prosperity that people are excluded from. Third, as moral yardsticks the views of democracy, equity, and diversity direct our discussion as to how and why the exclusion from different types of capital is harmful. Finally, tools of government represent four types of policy instrument, which local governments can use to eliminate or mitigate forms of exclusion. When various exclusion grounds coincide and opportunities to include groups and individuals become tenuous, one can speak of cumulative exclusion.

Keywords Exclusion ground • Types of capital • Moral yardsticks • Tools of government • Cumulative exclusion

TACKLING URBAN EXCLUSION

The popularity of the entrepreneurial and competition-oriented approaches to urban economic development increased and colored public policy interventions during the post-war decades, as pointed out in Chap. 2. Cities started to focus on attracting values and resources—most notably

© The Author(s) 2020
A.-V. Anttiroiko, M. de Jong, *The Inclusive City*,
https://doi.org/10.1007/978-3-030-61365-5_4

investments, talent, and tourists—from the outside world (Anttiroiko, 2015; de Jong et al., 2018; Florida, 2002; Landry, 2008). However, more recently the limits to this external orientation have come within sight, while clear signs emerged indicating that internal issues and endogenous aspects of urban development have come to the fore again. Demands for a safe city, resilient city, livable city, sharing city, and inclusive city grew increasingly strong and pressed urban governments to develop stronger social agendas (Schraven, Joss, & de Jong, 2020). Chapter 3 subsequently set out to define and circumscribe the various normative issues involved in the concepts of exclusion and inclusion and identified a number of dimensions needed in operationalizing inclusion. And while realizing a "just city" (Fainstein, 2010) implies a right to the city for all, it became fairly obvious that not all citizens of a given city can be included in each urban service or privileged position all of the time. Inclusiveness is much more complicated policy issue. In order to make sense of inclusion policy in the urban context, we need to drill deeper into who is excluded from what type of benefit or capital and on which grounds, and what kind of measures are deemed justifiable and feasible in each case in the pursuit of increasing the levels of inclusion.

A FRAMEWORK FOR ASSESSING THE EXCLUSIVENESS OF THE CITY

In this chapter, we will apply what was said in Chap. 3 regarding exclusion and inclusion in general terms to the urban context—as opposed to, for instance, the family, organizational, or national context. We will explore the various exclusion grounds and different types of capital (or access to opportunities to collect prosperity broadly defined) as they appear in cities, assess them in ethical terms, and examine what support structures urban governments could establish in the pursuit of higher levels of social and economic inclusiveness and what are the expected results of such interventions.

As prosperity entitlements, we have selected the five types of capital categorized in Chap. 3. It is important, however, to consider what these general categories mean at the local level. Human and cultural capital essentially refers to the appropriate honing, fostering, and use of knowledge and skills of citizens in the city, such as found in education, training, and cultural and sports facilities. Social capital is the development and maintenance of meaningful interpersonal networks in one's residential neighborhood or elsewhere in the city, both for career advancement and for other valued ways to spend time with fellow human beings. Citizens have sufficient amounts of financial capital at the urban level if the money value of their properties and regular income allows them to live a decent life and/or they have access to financial resources from banks at reasonable conditions for purchasing homes and other personal assets. With physical capital in cities, we mean constructed facilities in urban space used for a variety of crucial goods and services to citizens. These are primarily housing, work-related buildings such as factories and offices and various types of urban infrastructure services (transport, energy, waste management, water management, telecommunications, and internet). Finally, natural capital is comprised of all those natural resources that are or should be available to residents and users of urban space, such as fresh air, water, land, and greenery. We admit that this typology is not exhaustive. Rather, it construes the forms of capital that are most relevant for our purposes.

As moral yardsticks, we adopt the triptych democracy, equity, and diversity as proposed by Susan Fainstein in her book *The Just City* (Fainstein, 2010). With democracy, she essentially refers to broad citizen consultation and participation in decision-making on urban space as well as proportional representation across various strata, classes, and groups in urban society. With equity, she implies the presence of relative equality in levels of capital, income, and assets across these strata, classes, and groups and access to opportunities. Her interpretation of equity largely incorporates the various inclusion aspects highlighted in Chap. 3. Finally, she operationalizes diversity as the existence of genuine mutual recognition of various minority groups in the urban environment by their government as well as each other and their acting as legitimate players in decision-making processes.

As support structures, we have chosen the tools of government identified by Christopher Hood (1986), also known as policy instruments (de Bruijn & ten Heuvelhof, 1997), deployed by public authorities to influence the behavior of individual and private organizations in directions wished by those same authorities. Hood, whose typology we follow here, distinguishes four categories of tools:

- Nodality, which refers to instruments of knowledge and information collection (gathering data, intelligence, archiving, scientific studies) and dissemination (campaigns, promotion, advice, applied expertise) by governments.

- Authority, implying the application of legal and judicial measures to authoritatively intervene in societal phenomena and steer the options of natural and legal persons in a desired direction. Examples include legislation, permits, circulars, and legal decisions on individual cases. Some can restrict whereas others can expand the set of opportunities available to citizens.
- Treasure, the deployment of financial means to fix policy issues. This can take place either through collection of funds (taxation, contributions, fines, revenues from services delivered) or by means of (re) distribution of monetary sources from government to private players (subsidies, grants, discounts).
- Organization, which consists of physical and staffing aspects of policymaking and helps to bring various components of policymaking together in a consistent approach.

Since we will follow the list of various exclusion grounds from here on, their definition and operationalization will be dealt with underneath in the respective sub-sections. In practice, policy instruments tend to be used in various creative combinations to secure and/or reinforce their actual impact on actors' behavior. For example, a fine imposed on transgressing entities requires the legal foundation to impose it, the required information to establish a violation, and the staff to collect the data for this establishment.

AGE AS AN EXCLUSION GROUND

Among the various grounds for inclusion, age is comparatively speaking one of the least sensitive ones. In many instances, limitations to inclusion derive from official age restrictions. Young children may not have independent access to services and facilities because they are reliant on parental guidance, youngsters may not be entitled to certain legal options if they have not reached the age of 18, or elderly people may be obliged or entitled to retire over 65 or around that age (most Western countries have already increased flexibility regarding the retirement age). Both minors and elderly people may get discounts to certain municipal or other urban services, to which anyone between 18 and 65 will not be entitled. These age restrictions tend to be rarely disputed.

In a broader sense, however, we may also think of the simple availability of resources to boost human, social, and physical capital appropriate to various age groups. If the quantity or quality of primary and secondary schools and institutes for higher education is in short supply, this especially affects the opportunities of the young, while absence of geriatric hospitals has a negative impact on the well-being of seniors. If the availability of playgrounds, parks, or lifts in buildings is lacking, this may similarly affect the young or old disproportionately. If conversely the abovementioned types of capital are amply available, but transport modes primarily used by the working population or day care facilities on which they have to rely to have a carefree day at work are in short supply, this puts those in the working age brackets in a more difficult position.

In the broadest sense, lack of proportionality in the presence of various age groups in a city can be considered to reflect a low degree of inclusiveness. Should the elderly be overrepresented in the total population, for instance, one may consider that a potential problem that needs to be addressed. One could also reason in a different manner and argue that elderly people need a quieter social and physical environment and primarily wish to invest in developing social capital in their own age group. Adopting such an alternative line of reasoning would rather lead us to the conclusion that certain levels of non-inclusion would be the desirable outcome. Exclusion can in fact be a matter of choice as well.

Unless there are particular indications that in a given city, certain age groups are more involved or active in political and decision-making processes, the ethical requirement of democracy is not an important issue when it comes to age. The same applies to equity unless opportunities are very unevenly distributed across various age brackets in terms of access to any type of capital given their relative share of total population. The aspect of diversity perhaps deserves more attention in many cities in the developed world, given that on average immigrants tend to be younger than members of the autochthonous population and may have partially different needs, which may be or may not be adequately provided for. Conversely, it is well-known that most services to the elderly primarily target the original population and take their needs as a point of departure for delivery. Although they may well represent the lion's share of the elderly population, this percentage will decline in the coming decades and there are enough reasons to diversify the supply of various urban infrastructures and services to accommodate the needs of the elderly of non-Western origin, should such special needs arise.

Support structures favoring the inclusion of particular age groups (infants, youngsters, overburdened working parents, elderly) may be any of the four types. For instance, to protect the safety of young children in residential neighborhoods, both information campaigns for driving slowly or legal designations of a neighborhood as a Dutch-style "woonerf" (area where cars are only allowed to drive at walking speed) by means of formal road signs are conceivable. Likewise, similar measures can be implemented in areas where elderly homes are located. When it comes to elderly from ethnic minorities, public authorities may also want to collect information regarding their lifestyle-related wishes. The provision of organizational or financial measures makes at least as much sense to promote age-oriented inclusion. Organizational instruments can make public service staff available for counseling or service delivery or use the publicly-owned buildings to accommodate the special needs of the members of underrepresented age groups. Financial tools, on the other hand, may be deployed as subsidies for merit goods benefiting age groups by reducing their rates for a visit to a museum or theme park, or the use of subsidized taxi rides required to reach locations otherwise inaccessible. Often it will be a mixture of organizational and financial instruments that works best for activating different age groups among minorities when it is deemed legitimate and justified to include them in valued facets of urban life.

Physical and Mental Disabilities

Human disabilities to participate in public life come in many shapes and sizes. They can be physical or mental and lead to severe or light impairments. This variety makes it difficult to generalize on the necessity of government intervention to promote their inclusion. Although the topic of taking measures to promote their involvement in wider society is largely uncontested, this may be explained by the fact that their leverage to organize lobbies is comparatively weak. On the other hand, their disabilities have wide-ranging consequences for almost anything they can do in society. Most mental disabilities severely restrict the options to collect human capital and can only be partially compensated by sending people to special schools, which also tend to require special and intensive supervision. Likewise, the potential to develop a strong social network requires clear guidance. Since equally a far smaller range of job options is available to the mentally handicapped, their access to financial capital tends to be at the lower ends of the spectrum. Their access to housing, infrastructure services, and other types of physical capital depends on light or even heavy types of guidance and monitoring, with much the same applying to their use of natural capital.

Some of the same arguments apply to those having physical disabilities, although their potential to contribute economically is on average much higher through brainwork. Provided they enjoy practical support, they may be fully able to collect human capital in the education system or through cultural facilities in regular ways, develop social networks as strong as others, have access to financial capital, make use of physical capital, and breathe in the advantages of natural capital. Blind people may well be served by dogs trained to guide them through the streets and access many services in this manner, and individuals without legs will undoubtedly benefit from adjustments in various types of public infrastructures, such as in their homes, on buses, at railway stations, and various other places.

Offering the mentally impaired good quality care is relatively costly and societally inconspicuous, being thus primarily a matter of morality and ethics. Providing decent living standards to those born unlucky or permanently injured after grave accidents should perhaps be considered a sign of civilization. While diversity as a yardstick has little relevance here, equity (will they obtain a decent standard of living?) and democracy (to what extent are they offered a say in political or organizational affairs?) certainly matter. Different nations and cities are likely to make different choices in their trade-offs between efficiency and equity. The story for physical abilities is rather different. In many cases, the provision of support structures is likely to enable involved people to make considerable economic contributions to society, leading to rather different trade-offs between efficiency and equity in providing the help they need. Likewise, democratic participation may well be more within reach for them.

Regarding the application of support structures, legal instruments (protecting or delimiting certain rights and duties of handicapped and others toward each other) may involve formally requiring service providers to take minimum standards benefiting the handicapped into account, such as convenient entrance to the bus or the offering of Braille language for the blind in public places. Communicative instruments (collecting and disseminating information) can be used to inform the disabled of their possibilities and the broader audience to develop higher awareness of how the disabled experience public life. Financial and organizational instruments are certainly crucial too. Boosting the inclusion of the mentally and physically impaired primarily requires funding both as income support and as payment for facilities to help them function in daily life as well as the involvement of caretakers from health institutions. As mentioned before, it will often boil down to tailor-made packages of interventions coming from across the various types of support structures.

RELIGION, IDEOLOGY, RACE, AND ETHNICITY AS EXCLUSION GROUNDS

In many countries and cities, having been born into a particular religion, ideology, race, or ethnicity or converted to a particular religion or ideology does not or should not count as reason to exclude people from any type of relevant capital. It is a fact, however, that many countries—and consequently the cities within them—in authoritarian parts of the world have prevailing exclusionary arrangements. That said, also in liberal-democratic countries where freedom of religion and freedom of speech are widely proclaimed virtues and where most people (at least until the rise of the Black Lives Matter movement) believed discrimination was or should have been a thing of the past, one can easily recognize a smaller number of legal and potentially larger number of practical hurdles to full-scale inclusion of racial, ethnic, religious, and ideological minorities.

The most glaring legal barriers are the prohibition of memberships of fundamentalist or extremist strands within religions and ideologies aimed at sowing hate or destabilizing society or the state. More violent forms of Salafist and neo-Nazi groups come to mind first here. But probably far more contested are various forms of unspoken discrimination and hindrances in daily life experienced by moderate representatives of minority religions, especially when combined with distinguishable ethnic and racial features that make them stand out unmistakably from dominant white European or American populations. Many of these restrictions are formally non-existent and impermissible, but they do occur frequently, and their consequences become visible to any observer of urban life. In our further description, we will be focusing on the more subtle but still harmful forms of exclusion in cities in liberal-democratic nations.

When it comes to human and cultural capital, the main problems appear in the education system. Capabilities and qualities that minority children bring with them often tend to be underestimated by autochthonous teachers, leading them to lower their expectations or burden. They often have different sets of strengths and weaknesses than the regular white population and these may be undervalued by teachers or instructors. The line between genuine language delay and underestimation of capacity is crucial, but thin. Whether this picture extends to social capital too is related to the context in which people operate. This aspect is probably less relevant for children going to school but becomes all the more so when individuals develop personal and professional networks, which they need for their career advancement as adolescents and adults. "Old boys' networks" in companies still matter to a substantial degree for obtaining job promotions. These often operate on the basis of like-to-like associations in which the influence of ethnic, religious, and ideational affiliation is often more vital than publicly acknowledged. In such cases, being a self-declared follower of any religion or political ideology, such as being Christian or environmentalist, can work out in both favorable and unfavorable ways, depending on circumstances and the social circles relevant to the job at hand. Access to financial capital, on the other hand, is comparatively standardized and anonymized in the sense that there are relatively impartial standards for obtaining loans, subsidies, or paying fines and taxes. Their discriminatory impact is presumably smaller although definitely not nil. Especially when personal judgment is exerted by consultants or officials, impressions of people's appearance and mode of behavior come to the fore and affect the outcome of interactions, negotiations, estimations, and decisions. The same argumentation prevails, mutatis mutandis, to physical and natural capital: official differentiation based on religion or ideology is clearly forbidden and probably practically impossible or complicated when it comes to many types of facilities for housing, energy, transport, museums, or theme parks. On the other hand, when police surveillance officials in public parks on Sunday afternoon see immigrant communities having barbecues outside designated areas or failing to dispose their garbage at proper places, it is still up to their own personal discretion to establish whether they should encourage them to follow the rules, because "they still have to learn" or whether they should indeed be fined because they are citizens like anybody else and should therefore be treated accordingly. In urban space, important services or attractive natural resources are far more likely to be located in neighborhoods where communities raised and well-versed in the dominant religion or secular scientific worldview and (middle-of-the-road) political ideals reside than in minority quarters. This is rather the result of the interplay of various socio-economic factors correlated with racial, ethnic, religious, and ideological status than caused by outright and explicit exclusion. However, the impact of this amalgam of exclusionary practices can still be pervasive and lack of openness and inclusiveness toward minority groups in enjoying and participation in various aspects of urban prosperity are key to their quality of life experience. Cities that wish to be inclusive cannot afford to sit back when seeing such spatial segregation unfold in their midst.

In the realm of ethics, it is primarily diversity that should concern us. In principle, access in the city to any type of valuable capital should be evenly distributed across various ethnic and ideational groups. In practice, this is obviously often not present and in certain cases, especially where needs and preferences differ, variation across different groups and communities should even be provided. Adherents to the same religion may wish to live together in one district, surrounded by people and facilities suitable for or belonging to their own community. Whether urban policymakers accept or even applaud this as diversity across their urban space or see this as a menace leading to decreased levels of interaction across various communities differs per city. While some may propose a more even spread of population groups across the urban texture and seek to enact policy measures to counter ethnic fragmentation, others may feel that all deserve the freedom to live as and where they please. As Fainstein (2010) has pointed out, it is easy to overgeneralize in issues of diversity. Regarding equity and democracy, to the extent that there are problems of exclusion, these are often not the direct result of open racial, religious, or ideological discrimination. But they may well coincide with other exclusion grounds and then still have pernicious effects. In cities enjoying dominant left-liberal elites, such as Amsterdam or Stockholm, it is not uncommon to see patronizing attitudes toward white lesser-educated common people who apparently fail to understand how helpful immigration and cultural diversity are; it should be noted that these elites themselves tend to live in neighborhoods where few minority groups live, let alone cumulations of underprivileged ones.

Interventions with communicative policy instruments in this area primarily take the shape of collecting evidence on the presence and style of informal exclusionary practices in a given city, alongside the dissemination of information and raising of awareness among all citizens on how exclusion can be eliminated or mitigated at various levels. As mentioned above, in liberal democracies, legal measures to prevent exclusion and discrimination should theoretically not be necessary, but in practice inequalities persist and a lot of work remains to be done. There is simply a full legal ban on discrimination based on race, ethnicity, religion, or ideology and many nations and cities have anti-discrimination committees or ombudsmen in place where cases of abuse can be reported. Further inclusion may require firmer action. However, various forms of affirmative action such as adopting quotas for minority groups in job-hiring or temporary bans on the recruitment of male individuals are praised by some and despised by others, even among minority groups themselves. Alternatively, a radical leveling of the playing field through school and job application with anonymous assessment procedures to promote ethnic, religious, or other inclusion are increasingly frequently applied. Extremely contested are active policies to spread various minority groups across the city by pulling them out of their original ethnic enclaves to enhance inclusiveness throughout the city. These require a complex admixture of legal, financial, and organizational policy tools and historically the empirical results of such interventions appear mixed at best. Applying financial and organizational instruments can go as far as renovating neighborhoods, investing in a combination of community engagement and support of neighborhood-instigated surveillance activities, entertainment facilities, subsidized language training, and a variety of other initiatives none of which alone will suffice but the combination of which is likely to make a difference.

Gender and Sexual Identity

Much has been said and written about the inclusion of women, especially in the labor market. As in the above categories, gender-based inequality is widely rejected as morally objectionable and yet it persists. It is commonly assumed that men and women, homosexuals and heterosexuals are fully equivalent for performing virtually all tasks and should therefore be treated accordingly. In practice, in most countries and cities, men have traditionally occupied most of the top positions, tend to earn higher salaries, spend considerably less time inside their homes looking after the family and household, suffer less frequently from various forms of harassment, and enjoy easier access to professional circles or growth coalitions, where spoils are distributed. It is worth closer inspection to what extent such an asymmetry still holds in democratic societies, and if it does, what explains it, and further, how it manifests itself in the urban scene.

The acquisition of human capital by women and sexual minorities or the members of lesbian, gay, bisexual, transgender, queer/questioning, and intersex (LGBTQI) community seems barely to be impaired, given the fact that women in fact tend to perform better within the education system than men do. With regard to sexual minorities, the evidence is more mixed, but if anything, one can conclude that the education system in European and American cities favors women over men, which raises questions on the prevalence of teaching methods and female teachers at school. As regards social capital on the other hand, a very different picture emerges. Men spend more time on social activities and community life than women do, at least partly because of gender-biased patterns of parenting and caring at home. Since they are also more active and ambitious in job acquisition, the positive bias for women in their access to human capital is reversed for social capital: women are better educated, but men tend to get the better-paid jobs. Wherever husband and wife live together in good harmony within the family their access to financial capital may look the same, but as soon as they live as singles or experience the pain of divorce differences emerge. Women tend to have lower incomes and have a higher chance of being socio-economically deprived when raising children. Men, while enjoying higher levels of income, often pay substantial amounts of alimony for ex-partners or children depending on the institutional conditions that prevail in the nation and city in question. Finally, access to and use of physical and natural capital will only diverge across the two sexes to the extent that they reflect time spent in or around them for reasons noted above.

The situation for sexual minorities is different in the sense that in the absence of formal exclusion or discrimination at times their public appearance or official display of their identity can be reason for harassment or even physical attacks. The most liberal and open of European cities have been reported to have such assaults with regular intervals. Different members of the LGBTQI community may clearly react differently to these challenges, but the very consideration of these dangers may often make them feel less secure and this already goes to the detriment of having an open and inclusive city. Things even get worse if they get harassed around their house when intolerant and violent neighbors know about their lifestyle and are determined to force them to move elsewhere. This makes social exclusion even more explicitly of a delicate urban issue that should be handled with fervor and care.

For gender and sexual identity, the moral yardsticks of democracy, equity, and diversity all matter to some extent. If women are underrepresented in political and organizational life, especially at the top, the inclusive democracy as an ideal is at stake. If their career opportunities are inferior to those of men in spite of equal or even superior education levels, equity is under attack. And if members of the LGBTQI community in practice cannot feel free to present themselves openly in public events even though formally they should be, diversity is impaired. But what policy measures are conceivable to improve the fate of the inclusive city?

Among the tools of government, the communicative ones could make a limited contribution through public campaigns raising awareness, even though they alone are unlikely to produce satisfactory results. Legal equality has long been in place, but this is not reflected in daily urban life. On this count, much the same applies to ethnic and religious minorities: affirmative action is conceivable and may indeed work to increase representation of women and sexual minorities in key places, but this may go to the detriment of this segment if the ones being favored by this system are perceived as underperforming in their role. Another option is the legal requirement to radically equalize remuneration for women in the same functions as men working for the municipal government (e.g., standard pay agreements). Such regulations are in place in many liberal countries. Since this has financial implications, this would effectively be a combination of legal and financial policy instruments promoting gender inclusion. Deploying organizational resources for the benefit of women and sexual minorities is ineffectual, given that they do not live in separate neighborhoods, do not require specific urban infrastructures or housing services, or suffer from educational disadvantages. Their problematique is clearly of a different nature than that of cultural minorities.

INCOME AND WEALTH

If there is any central factor being of central impact to the limitations people experience to be included in all types of capital available in the city, this must be money. In many ways, it acts as a catalyst for the other exclusion grounds. Both inherited and earned wealth open up enormous opportunities to improve a person or family's social capital (although for newcomers there is perhaps a risk of being accused to act like an upstart), acquire more financial capital and find residence in most desirable neighborhoods with good housing and access to high-quality infrastructures and unbeatable scenery and natural resources. Although having the disposal of enough funds does not directly give access to any educational degree one might want (university degrees are normally not for sale) or to any type of political business function of importance, at least theoretical access to the opportunity to study under high-quality supervision or enjoy the benefits of world-class museums anywhere in the world are within reach. Conversely, however, for those lacking such sources of income and wealth, the odds are that this penury often comes together with other types of exclusion grounds of which disabilities, ethnic backgrounds, and educational qualifications are often the most notable ones. Still, the impact of levels of income and wealth on exclusion from various types of capital present in the city needs to be examined on its own terms.

Low-income individuals and households are not necessarily directly excluded from human and cultural capital. However, the indirect consequences of poverty are evident: in most countries and cities, having one's residence in particular areas determine accessibility of high-quality schools, although active government intervention on various fronts can weaken this phenomenon. The same applies, albeit that the impact of this is far more limited, to facilities boosting one's cultural capital, such as museums and concert halls. In the growing selection of places where higher education requires extensive amounts of financial input from parents, exclusionary practices even work directly: children in low-income groups need to borrow substantial loans from banks to get access to universities or polytechnics, and occasionally this may even be beyond their reach. When looking at social capital, money talks in different ways: to the extent that having limited financial resources available still allows people to participate in various communities where valuable personal and professional networks can be built, the impact of money on acquiring at least medium social capital will be negligible. This will be mostly the case in egalitarian societies where public services are in ample supply. But in cities where one's attractiveness is heavily determined by family capital and well-paid positions that relatives have, the options tend to be far more restricted. Most people will judge others by the families they grew up in, the schools they have been to, the neighborhoods where they live, and the friends they have collected over time. Under such conditions, gaps in wealth are amplified in the acquisition of human and social capital and many types of exclusion reinforce each other. The remainder of the story extending to financial capital, physical capital, and natural capital is then fairly easily told. Having large financial reserves facilitates further rent-seeking and good opportunities at the capital market or the possibility to obtain good advice for wise investments or bank loans. This also makes it possible to find or keep one's residence in privileged neighborhoods with good facilities and one is based in close proximity to attractive natural spaces. Working-class and service-class families are clearly missing out on most of these advantages, while people in the middle and creative classes may be included in some, but not in other types of capital. It may partly depend on strategies and partly on chance factors how their lives will unfold.

In more minimalistic conceptions of representative democracy à la Schumpeter, wide income gaps do not matter much: anybody can vote. However, when one is striving for more generous and comprehensive forms of public participation, having enough money resources obviously does matter for being included in decision-making. This is even more true for aspects of equity, which almost by definition imply that smaller gaps between rich and poor result in more equitable cities. In terms of diversity, the decision criterion would be whether there is a large overlap between low-income groups and communities of non-dominant racial, ethnic, religious, ideological, or other backgrounds. If the latter is the case, we could speak of high levels of diversity exclusion.

Since wealth and income policies cut at the heart of economic allocation and distribution in societies, it is primarily the national government which is at the rudder for selecting instruments to increase levels of inclusiveness. What local governments can do to reduce socio-economic inequality is to adopt regulation that forces off the mixing of income groups in using public services such as schools or residential facilities, to maximize the open access of all income groups to all parts of town, applying tax and subsidy policies that benefit lower-income groups on various counts, and to offer people from low-income groups extra protection by making more local government staff available in their favor. Again, it is often an intelligent mixture of such policy instruments that may produce the best results. Communicative instruments, however, can only be a useful information add-on to the others, but are unlikely to create much in and by themselves.

LOCATION AS AN EXCLUSION GROUND

Formal residence is not a contested criterion for being included to or excluded from eligibility for certain urban services and conveniences. Some facilities in large cities, such as public transport, museums, or ferryboats, are accessible to anyone; others may be free or accessible only to nationals, while some may be only available to locals. Those living in a city can reap the sweet fruits of having official residence there, while others who pay their municipal taxes elsewhere should claim their benefits wherever they have their legally recognized residence. Some urban governments may be richer and charge lower taxes and/or offer better urban infrastructures than others, but skewness can in this regard barely be interpreted as a lack of inclusiveness. This picture changes when it comes to locations being of practical convenience or inconvenience. What if there are systematically more cash dispensers present in favored parts of town, or maintenance of pavements diverges noticeably across neighborhoods? What if bus services are lacking and taxis avoid offering their services in areas reputed to be unsafe, while being amply available in hyped quarters where roads are covered by the shadows of luscious palm-trees? Each location tells a different story, the other end being that of privileged neighborhoods that indeed welcome exclusionary practices in order to maintain their reputation of luxury and other aspects of their status quo, while even the mere presence of those coming from deprived areas is frowned on.

First, location matters to human capital through access to primary schools. In many cities acceptance at schools is dependent on the area where people live. If it is not, an inconvenient commute still remains as a lasting headache for those who wish to take their children to popular educational institutions. This aspect decreases in importance for secondary and higher education, although there the aspect of having longer travel times remains for people living in small communities situated out of town. Since, as we observed above, social capital grows in importance later than human capital, limitations derived from location decrease in relative importance over time: next of kin, friends, and colleagues may be further removed than for those living in ex-centric locations, but this hurdle can be overcome or may be the logical consequence of living a comfortable suburban or ex-urban existence further away from downtown areas. Location as an exclusion ground in terms of financial capital can play an important role when this affects the value of one's properties negatively or when the availability or price of financial or insurance services are influenced by one's location and its reputation. And finally, as for human and social capital, access to or use of physical and natural capital may be (partly) impaired by one's living in underprivileged or rural locations. To sum up, where inclusion issues due to location coincide with other exclusion grounds, they may represent cumulative inequality. If not, they may well be the result of conscious choices to live somewhere.

Ethically, the yardstick of democracy is not seriously influenced by location other than that people who have residence are likely to be only entitled to suffrage and direct participation (as beneficiary) in decision-making concerning the election district in which they live. The equity argument would only be relevant in case of cumulative inequalities due to various exclusion grounds occurring at the same time, but not if living in an excentric location is the result of intentional behavior. The same argument applies to diversity. If any types of minorities mostly and systematically reside in areas where various facilities are absent or of low quality, this would hint at consistent exclusionary practices harming specific communities and would be a clarion call for government action.

Before addressing the question which support structures can be put in place to promote the inclusion of people at disadvantaged location, we should point out that we will only mention the non-cumulative forms of exclusion here, since the cumulative ones have already been amply described above. To raise levels of inclusion for location, the use of communicative instruments is not particularly relevant. Authority, or legal instruments, can be fruitfully used if the goal is to balance rights and duties: in such cases, a clear circumscription of those who are entitled to municipal services and who are not can be legitimately made on the basis of who have a legal obligation to pay local taxes or who reside permanently in the jurisdiction. Conversely, if the aim is to include non-local citizens in urban service delivery, legal provisions should be made to grant such an entitlement. The latter is for instance practiced by generous Chinese municipalities who enlarge their service delivery to working migrants who do not hold the right household papers ("hukou") for their city. Complementing the above legal instruments can then be "treasure," financial sources, or monetary compensation made available to those who do not hold local citizenship or who live far out of town, for instance by subsidizing the construction of local roads or bus transport services for them. Finally, organization can be provided as a fourth type of policy instrument by offering decentralized government services in suburban or ex-urban locations to make them available to the small numbers of households in the country-side.

CHALLENGES IN RESPONDING TO VARIOUS FORMS OF EXCLUSION

Although some types of exclusion happen to certain social groups at the same time and can therefore be considered cumulative forms of exclusion requiring strong coordinated action, other forms of exclusion do not coincide or may even work against each other. Offering extra local transport services to those living out of town may indeed have a de-leveling effect if these rural inhabitants happen to be well-earning individuals. If safe havens are to be provided to members of the LGBTQI community at a low cost but these happen to land in conservative Christian or Muslim neighborhoods where open displays of homosexuality are frowned on or wish to work at religious schools where the management or concerned parents have moral objections against gay teachers, not all inclusion and diversity claims can be granted at the same time. And finally, when local political parties strive for equal representation of men and women among their councilors or a proportional distribution of highly and average educated backbenchers at the same time, it sometimes happens that they have to make choices in favor of one type of inclusion and against another. Although Hambleton (2015) does well to propose that inclusive cities should stringently offer democracy, equity, and diversity all at the same time, reality tells us that this happens only rarely. More often painful choices have to be made. Chapters 5 and 6 on inclusion policy and governance issues will delve more deeply into the challenges involved in making these trade-offs between various types of inclusion.

References

Anttiroiko, A.-V. (2015). *The Political Economy of City Branding*. London: Routledge.

de Bruijn, H., & ten Heuvelhof, E. (1997). Instruments for Network Management. In W. J. M. Kickert, E.-H. Klijn, & J. F. M. Koppenjan (Eds.), *Managing Complex Networks: Strategies for the Public Sector* (pp. 166–191). London: Sage.

de Jong, M., Chen, Y., Joss, S., Lu, H., Zhao, M., Qihui Yang, Q., et al. (2018). Explaining City-Branding Practices in China's Three Mega-City Regions: The Role of Ecological Modernization. *Journal of Cleaner Production, 179*, 527–543.

Fainstein, S. S. (2010). *The Just City*. Ithaca: Cornell University Press.

Florida, R. (2002). *The Rise of the Creative Class: And How it's Transforming Work, Leisure, Community and Everyday Life*. New York: Perseus Book.

Hambleton, R. (2015). *Leading the Inclusive City: Place-based Innovation for a Bounded Planet*. Bristol, UK: Policy Press.

Hood, C. (1986). *The Tools of Government*. London: Chatham House Publishers.

Landry, C. (2008). *The Creative City; A Toolkit for Urban Innovators*. London: Routledge.

Schraven, D., Joss, S., & de Jong, M. (2020). Past, Present and Future: Engagement with Sustainable Urban Development through 35 city Labels in the Research Literature 1990–2019. Under review in: *Journal of Cleaner Production*.

CHAPTER 5

Policymaking for Inclusive Cities

Abstract Before inclusive urban development can be truly implemented as a policy direction by local governments, a number of preconditions have to be met. One of them is a constructive handling of the tensions as they emerge between groups that have divergent identities. As people have various memberships in groups that form a part of an individual's multidimensional identity, they imply diverging forms and levels of exclusion, referred to as intersectionality. If gaps between identity groups are substantial and identity groups overplay the role of such differences, the resulting cleavages should be addressed through inclusive policymaking where local government is capable of scrutinizing such tensions, showing overarching leadership, and creating a unifying policy vision and framework.

Keywords Identity • Intersectionality • Value trade-off • Inclusion • Policymaking • Leadership

THE COMPLEXITY OF INCLUSIVE URBAN DEVELOPMENT

This chapter discusses the preconditions to be taken into account in the making of policies favoring inclusive urban development. Even if promoting inclusive urban development appears at first sight a policy agenda that will meet with broad approval and goodwill among local residents and their political representatives, realizing it is not always that

© The Author(s) 2020
A.-V. Anttiroiko, M. de Jong, *The Inclusive City*,
https://doi.org/10.1007/978-3-030-61365-5_5

straightforward. First, as with any other policy issue, there is usually more than one legitimate interpretation of the reasons, justifications, and effects of any particular form of exclusion and of the required corrective actions proposed as remedies. The issue and its possible fixes may also be politically sensitive. Second, the more fine-grained a view we have of specific forms of exclusion and the complexity of its interrelatedness with various policy areas and the impacts of measures undertaken, the more difficult it is to offer simple solutions that do not affect other groups. Third, as important as individual and group-specific rights can be, they should be understood as an integral part of a complete set of municipal policies and as a component of the wider framework within which a moral polity operates.

Each individual policy solution has a connection with a host of controversial issues, which relate to individual responsibilities, value incompatibilities, feasibility issues, and unintended consequences. Many of them boil down to the fact that good intentions of identity groups, politicians, or public managers to change things for the better do not automatically translate into positive outcomes. The tension that exists between developing an inclusive city as an end and the means by which this should be realized demonstrate the above difficulty. When it comes to as elusive a phenomenon as inclusive urban prosperity, the fundamental policymaking challenge is the difficulty to determine the desired end without ambiguity, which implies that the justification of policy measures face similar challenges. The premises and design of building an inclusive city require careful socio-philosophical analysis as well as the exposing of value judgments and ethical considerations.

IDENTITIES, INTERSECTIONALITY, AND THE TRADE-OFFS OF INCLUSION

In the previous chapter, we elaborated on a number of critical dimensions in exclusion and made remarks on how these can be addressed. They were discussed as separate manifestations of exclusion. Our next step is to bring them together as interrelated issues subject to contestation in urban policymaking.

Societies—or urban communities for that matter—where particularistic views and sectional interests are emphasized, as it tends to happen when groups with distinct identities multiply and their agendas become pronounced, are subject to growing fragmentation and instability. This tendency was strengthened in the aftermath of the assumed triumph of liberal democracy (Fukuyama, 1992). The latter was supposed to liberate individuals from collective ties and enable them to cultivate their own lifestyles instead of making them mere pawns in the ideological struggles that emanate from grand narratives (Mouffe, 2005). Instead, what emerged around the turn of the millennium was something quite different, as epitomized by the rise of increasingly sensitive, divisive, and destructive identity politics (Furedi, 2019).

A critical turning point was the emergence of radical movements of the 1960s, which set the ball rolling in the new direction. The working-class movement addressed "classism" or material inequality, early feminism demanded gender equality, and the civil rights movement fought against racial discrimination, all attempting to correct glaring injustices that were centrifugal forces in society. This was the time of "good" identity politics (Haidt, 2017). In the decades that followed, however, discussions radicalized especially in academia, opening up an ever-diversifying field of identities, each reflecting their sense of victimhood, sensitivities, and particularistic political objectives, and this led to an increasingly divided political landscape. Group-consciousness turned into inherently exclusionary group-centeredness. Increased sensitivity seems to have risen in parallel with the growing influence of new generations—the Millennials and Generation Z—and, equally importantly, with the impact of social media, which has increased polarization, wokeness, explicit judgment and rejection of others, and a kind of cancel culture. This eventually made it increasingly challenging to develop consensus on any policies (Haidt, 2017; Haidt & Rose-Stockwell, 2019).

These politically significant identities vary in terms of controversiality, intransigence, and influence in political arenas and in the media. The victims of racism, sexism, transgender oppression, and heterosexism are clearly most visible in the current discourse on identity, while religious oppression and classism have obtained a somewhat lower status followed by ableism and ageism. As individuals, people do not represent only one group nor are they necessarily subject to only one type of oppression, discrimination, or exclusion. That implies that exclusion can take place simultaneously on various grounds and in different forms. For example, a disabled black lesbian woman may be oppressed in four different aspects. Another example is people of color (POC) in the LGBTQI community, who are not only discriminated against because of their sexual orientation but may also experience racism within their own minority groups (Cyrus, 2017). This phenomenon has been labeled as intersectionality, which in its original formulation by Kimberlé Crenshaw (1989) contains an insightful message (Adams & Bell, 2016). When this scheme is taken beyond its original scope, however, it entails that we all represent actually almost indefinite number of dimensions that constitute our personal and social identities, of which we benefit or suffer in varying degrees, be it looks, physical health, height, weight, hair, age, race, sex, religion, wealth, temperament, mental health, education, intelligence, or any other consideration. This puts the inclusion agenda in perspective and makes it extremely challenging to handle. Moreover, at the same time it is evident that the ultimate assessment of the "hierarchy" of an individual's multilayered identities is subjective and must be, thus, primarily dealt with at the individual level. In such settings, the importance of tolerance and endurance in the city can barely be overestimated, and local governments would do well to promote antidotes against hypersensitivity.

In addition, when such views instigate us to see the world through dichotomous lenses, that is, privileges versus oppression, or simply good against bad, and when particular identity aspects are rated above the merits of individuals, views of exclusion and inclusion begin to lose their credibility.

Intragroup and Intergroup Cleavages

The problem with particularistic identity politics is that while it is supposed to improve the position of the members of various groups, it actually stresses distinctions between people. Instead of seeing each person as a unique individual, it perceives him or her through an antagonistic lens, only as a member of an identity group. Rarely do identity groups explicitly aim at including themselves and excluding others, but their promotion of group interests, and paradoxically, demand for special treatment in a tolerant multicultural context, turns occasionally their exclusion into a privilege from which others can be excluded. Consequently, each of these groups benefit from overplaying "difference" in order to gain recognition, entitlements, and influence. While their challenge to nationalist, traditionalist, localist, and conservative views creates an inevitable political battlefield, such multiple identities inevitably breed incompatibility and tension within local communities and for local governments. These tensions may arise even within each identity group. For example, some lesbians have been criticized by other segments of the LGBTQI community for being too restrictive with anchoring understanding of what it means to be a lesbian on a biologically grounded view of a woman. Many of those who suffer from gender dysphoria can actually be victims of allegations from transgender activists, who advocate only one view of a complex issue. The white feminists of the 1960s have been said to actually enjoy their "white privilege" according to proponents of radical black feminism. Ethnic minorities can also be treated differently, as in the case of affirmative action in higher education in the USA, which favors African Americans and sets Asian Americans at a clear disadvantage.

Intergroup tensions emerge when different identity groups represent diverse values, cultures, priorities, or political views. Among religious groups, the increased role of Islam in the Western countries has raised multiple issues in which it seems to be in conflict with feminism and LGBTQ rights and more generally with Western rationalism, liberal values, and certain aspects of internationally recognized human rights. There are also issues of entitlements, prerogatives, and benefits, which are inherent sources of conflict between different social classes or generations.

To sum up, when promoting inclusive urban development, policymakers will have to handle rising levels of tensions between various social groups, especially where they have adopted separate and potentially exclusionary identities, make trade-offs within broader contexts of exclusion and inclusion, and demonstrate leadership in buttressing these trade-offs in a broader vision of their inclusive city. To what extent can members of religious groups participate if they do not share women's rights? How do policymakers deal with impoverished white working-class people who declare themselves explicitly anti-Muslim? Can certain groups of underprivileged indigenous people or the people of color be provided easier access to universities than other ethnic minorities or white people from poor neighborhoods? Can it be justified that senior people with generous pensions get theater or train tickets at considerable discounts while financially tight street cleaners do not? Should the use of men's or women's toilets and locker rooms be based on biological differences (gender binary) or on subjective gender identity? There are countless issues that potentially justify special treatment, but local policymakers are in dire need to establish broader and well-reflected overarching visions on how to deal with distinctions between and within social groups, how to balance these, and how to warrant them within their democratic and rule-of-law-based decision-making systems.

BOLSTERING THE INCLUSIVE CITY THROUGH HANDLING DIVISIVENESS

The tensions described above do not make realizing the inclusive city an unachievable ideal. Rather, policymakers in the inclusive city must adopt approaches and design policies that take such biases into account and balance them against each other in the policymaking process. First, divisiveness must be eased with an integrative approach based on a city's vision, community-level objectives, and values. Urban governments are capable of delivering better results when acting as a unifying force, rather than when serving as a handling center of sectional interests. They should prioritize those excluded groups that are considered in most urgent need and assess such policies within a wide framework that aims at the well-being of all members of the community. This requires that the issues of exclusion and inclusion are dealt with within sound and strong place-based leadership in which shared values and visions are clearly articulated, local interests carefully traded off against each other, various types of capital owned by different groups and individuals utilized, partnerships developed, and social cohesion maintained (Hambleton, 2015).

Moreover, local governments have a responsibility of widening the agenda from rights and benefits to responsibilities, value creation, and opportunity enhancement. Their task is to ensure justified deregulation or reregulation measures in their drive for inclusion and balanced allocation of resources to different groups, all on the basis of an analytical and value-sensitive evaluation of their needs. While doing so, existing policies and practices are to be reviewed in order to ensure that they do not include unjustified exclusionary elements as side-effects of fragmented inclusionary policies.

While some interests are voiced by loud advocates, it is good to remember that there are aspects of exclusion that are not expressed in the political agenda, and that the consequences of exclusion may surge at times in the form of apathy or anti-social behavior. A representative case of the latter is the destruction of educational facilities or libraries by members of disadvantaged communities at their own peril (e.g., Stilwell, 2016).

Another extremely important message is that rather than imposing a specific interpretation of the globalized progressive agenda (Mouffe, 2005), which can sometimes be experienced as patronizing to one or more groups in the local community, there is a need to listen to the members of these social groups and co-create solutions with them, rather than mastermind programs relying on ideas of the political elite and administrative machinery. For example, regarding the evaluation of inclusionary education policies in Australia, Smyth (2010) concluded that there is a need to include the voices of "policy users," who are supposed to be the beneficiaries, in the construction of reflexive alternatives. In addition, an ever-present danger with bureaucratically scaled-up social inclusion initiatives—like the ministerial Flexible Learning Options (FLO) student enrollment strategy to assist schools in supporting young people who have disengaged from school in Australia—is that such initiatives become a parallel "safety-net" education system for the disadvantaged and thereby corrode the principle of an inclusive mainstream education system meeting the needs of all children and young people (Bills, Armstrong, & Howard, 2020).

Such messages emphasize the need to look beyond sectional interests and refocus on the empowerment side of the picture. This strategy has most potential when not only purely identity-based group interests are heeded, even though these are usually most controversial ones, but also groups formed around age or disability, which are less vocal but quite often at least as much in need. In order to avoid adopting a patronizing attitude, policymakers should (i) listen to the members of the excluded groups, (ii) involve all relevant stakeholders in policymaking process, (iii) empower target groups and their organizations, and (iv) adjust mainstream arrangements on the basis of the democratic dialogue. Factual arrangements depend, of course, on the form and nature of exclusion, characteristics of the group, and the nature, scope, and urgency of the policy issue in question in the given context (see, e.g., Smith, 2019).

A Framework for Urban Inclusion Policy

In order for an inclusive city to be resilient, healthy, and vibrant, it needs to go beyond a rights-oriented view and embrace the opportunity-oriented side of inclusion. If developed in an integrative and holistic manner, rights and opportunities may actually feed each other, for inclusion has a potential to strengthen local capital and its utilization for development, while economic growth in turn tends to strengthen demands for democracy and inclusion. Related to this, effective inclusion reduces the need for group-based identity politics, which again helps to bring people together as individuals rather than as representatives of particular identities. This, in turn, further improves conditions for synergistically creating social and economic value.

The latter is good news for economic inclusion, since in its paradigmatic form it is all about opening new horizons of economic opportunities to underserved social groups. It is based on the idea of equality of opportunity and the full utilization of human potential in the conditions of an open society. As defined by the European Bank for Reconstruction and Development, "[a]n inclusive market economy ensures that anyone regardless of their gender, place of birth, socio-economic environment, age or other circumstances has full and fair access to labour markets, finance and entrepreneurship and, more generally, economic opportunity" (EBRD, 2017, p. 5). The idea is that the economic institutions, markets, and education systems should enhance economic opportunities to individuals regardless of their backgrounds or specific circumstances. It requires not only that legal frameworks, institutions, and policies are free from bias but in a more active sense seeking to reduce barriers to participation in the economy (EBRD, 2017, p. 10).

The policymaking process starts from setting the agenda and conducting analyses, including political demands, problem identification, an evidence-based view of exclusion, an examination of both the causes and effects of exclusion, and the assessment of unused potential in various corners of the city. This process entails more than policy formulation and the planning of policy interventions based on a rule of thumb. In order to provide a sharp and analytical view of the issues, one option is to apply the COM-B system in analyzing human behavior and the Behavior Change Wheel to connect it with policy categories (Michie, van Stralen, & West, 2011). The COM-B scheme facilitates our understanding of how capacity (C), opportunity (O), and motivation (M) affect behavior (B), which in turn condition intervention functions (restricting, persuading, incentivizing, training), and can then be formulated as relevant policy categories, such as planning, communication, legislation, service provision, regulation, fiscal measures, and guidelines. A simplified policymaking scheme is depicted in Fig. 5.1.

A policy for creating an inclusive city is often portrayed as political issue with unproblematic view of identities or interests. But as shown above, it is actually often a thorny process where various trade-offs are to be made and controversies handled. Even more importantly, it must be based on a democratic, responsible, and integrative approach, which (a) is based on empirical evidence and impartial analyses, (b) balances different interests, and (c) brings all separate interests together under a cohesive and

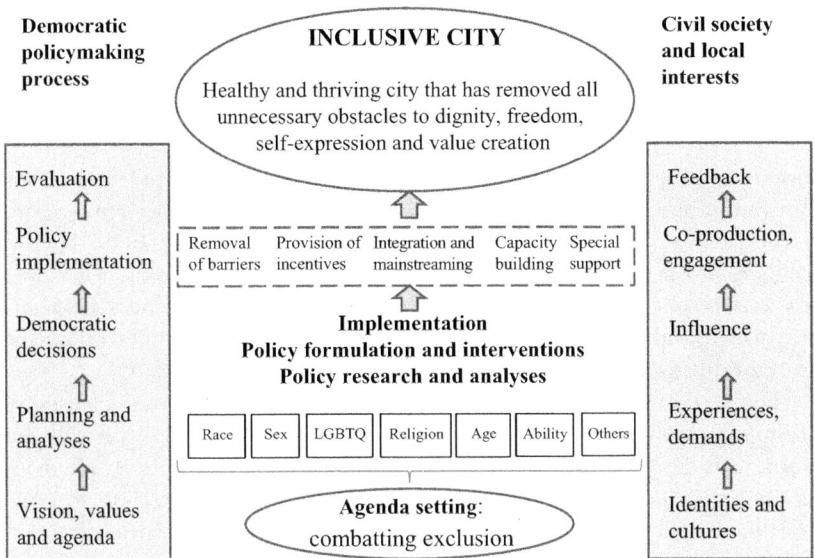

Fig. 5.1 Policymaking for inclusive cities

integrative umbrella. Local government needs to pay attention to the continuum of policy intervention functions, which invoke *personal agency*, such as education, persuasion, incentivization, training, and enablement, while other functions, such as modeling (based on our propensity to imitate), environmental restructuring (adopting to the demands of the social, political, and economic environments), restriction, and coercion, place more emphasis on *external influences* (Michie et al., 2011). To generalize, city-wide rights-based inclusion relies primarily on the removal of obstacles in the name of the equality of opportunity, while special structural asymmetries or injustices invoke long-term capacity-building programs, regulation, or favorable conditions. A step forward from here is to consider opportunities for utilizing inclusion as a means for contributing to the prosperity of urban communities, which will be addressed next.

STRATEGIES FOR CO-CREATED SHARED URBAN PROSPERITY

Problems of social and economic exclusion are so obvious and well-documented that we have not devoted much space to discuss them here. However, when turning our attention from a one-dimensional and particularistic rights-oriented view toward a value creation and more visionary, holistic, and integrative view of inclusion, a few additional remarks are in order. That is, there are several groups in society which do not harness their full potential in creating and capturing value due to lack of capacity, motivation, or opportunity. It is thus a win-win game to empower all segments of the community and strengthen both urban economy and community livability (on the foundations of inclusive prosperity and capitalism, see, e.g., Jacobs & Mazzucato, 2016; Lee, 2019; Naidu, Rodrik, & Zucman, 2019). Creating high-quality opportunities for workers and businesses, increasing economic mobility, narrowing significant disparities, and developing cities as the loci of high quality of life are means to shared prosperity (Berube, Bosland, Greene, & Rush, 2018).

The first strategic issue is to use all possible means to enhance equality of opportunity and, especially, to improve the economic position of the poor, as it has a very direct positive impact on urban growth. Apart from opportunity, people must also have the capacity and motivation to contribute, which poses a challenge when groups are not sufficiently integrated in the rest of the urban community. Public-sector organizations are in a key position to create favorable conditions for such a development, including both their inclusionary policies as employers and inclusiveness as the fundamental value that characterizes their governance style (OECD, 2015).

In most cities in developed countries, women are already well represented in public organizations. However, there is still room for improvement in their role in entrepreneurship (female entrepreneurs represent some one-third of the self-employed in the European Union) and management and professional occupations in the private sector. This requires capacity building, motivation, and incentivization designed for women. In the same vain, both ethnopreneurship and the integration of ethnic minorities into the mainstream economy may require special encouragement on the part of local institutions. Ageism should be tackled due to its negative impact on the old-age dependency ratio as well as the unused potential of senior citizens. Thus, literally among all excluded groups in society potential can be unleashed through inclusionary policies, in order to increase their economic participation, offer them better chances to contribute to society, and pave the way for mainstreaming economic inclusion. Such a process does not happen overnight on the basis of some authoritative government decisions, but rather is a long-term transformation process. It requires efforts to empower all relevant segments of society and provide them access to policy and decision processes. It is supposed to ensure that the needs and aspirations of various groups are taken into account, while at the same time balanced and synthesized through value-driven leadership of local government (OECD, 2015). This setting is illustrated in Fig. 5.2.

A number of policy areas stand out in functioning as entry points to realizing long-term urban inclusive prosperity. A crucial precondition for being able fully to harness the capacity, opportunity, and motivation of disadvantaged people is a large-scale *poverty alleviation*. National and local governments have several tools to reduce income inequality, including (1) tax and social transfer policies, (2) employment policies and policies affecting the wage-bargaining process, (3) in-kind benefits through public services and spending for education, health, and other important services, (4) regulatory levers such as reducing barriers to accessing economic opportunity, and (5) strengthening the rule of law, reducing special statuses or loopholes, and ensuring inclusive policy development processes and effective policy implementation (OECD, 2015).

Another set of actions addresses the spatial aspects of exclusion. Local governments should pay attention to inclusiveness of urban structures (e.g., Transit Oriented Development and availability of public spaces), infrastructures and utilities, housing, and safety. Urban planning is vital for

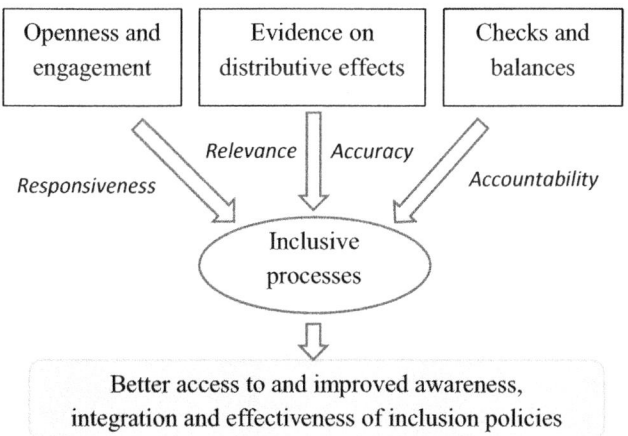

Fig. 5.2 Key elements of an inclusive policymaking process. (Source: Modified from OECD, 2015)

promoting inclusiveness in the city. *Inclusive urban infrastructure develop-ment* is an integrated approach encompassing sustainable, resilient, accessible, and affordable solutions to the challenges faced by the urban poor and vulnerable groups through enhancing their access to urban services and infrastructure through targeted investments (ADB, 2017).

A third content-related precondition for inclusive economic development is the full utilization of urban transformative capacity, institutional thickness, and local capitals in building the inclusive city. This includes the creation of partnerships that are essential in both creating synergies by bringing all the available resources to support inclusion policy and ascertain that they are optimally used within the integrative whole-of-government framework (OECD, 2015). The integrated approach utilizes institutional delivery mechanisms that bring together all institutions and stakeholders that have the capacity to contribute to the inclusive urban service delivery and other aspects of inclusive urbanism (ADB, 2017).

Building on such preconditions, local governments can sharpen the focus on the co-creation of shared urban prosperity, in which the issues of intersectionality with regard to race, class, gender, sexuality, age, and ability are brought together in terms of intervention functions in order to optimize their ability to bring value to the urban community. The previous discussion aims to point out that in order for special inclusionary measures to be successful, there has to be a fruitful soil for their utilization. For example, eradication of extreme poverty is essential in fighting against apathy and alienation. Similarly, creating inclusive urban space increases the opportunity of utilizing the resources available in our socio-economic environment.

Strategies for urban value creation include (a) access to skills and employment, (b) entrepreneurship and access to finance, and (c) access to services that enhance economic opportunities (EBRD, 2017). These elements are illustrated in Fig. 5.3.

Access to skills and employment is needed to diversify workforce, tap into talent pools, retain and up-skill staff, and improve R&D capacity. Such efforts start by increasing the availability of skilled labor and enhancing local training and work-based learning opportunities in partnership with education institutions. Inclusive policies can be executed via platforms that bring together employers and education authorities to address the issues relating to national skill standards and expected future labor market needs. Such an approach aims to strengthen the employability of disadvantaged groups and enhance equitable access to high skills through improved

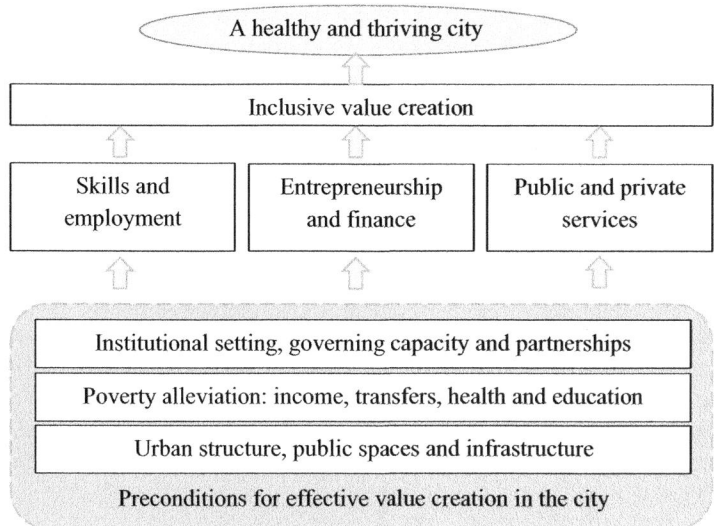

Fig. 5.3   Aspects of inclusive economic development policy

facilities and offerings via capacity building, training of trainers, and designing incentive programs to educational institutions. Local governments can also promote equal opportunities both in public- and private-sector organizations, including indirect symbolic measures that encourage private-sector-driven mainstreaming through a Diversity and Inclusion (D&I) approach that promote variegated input to the workforce and supply chains (see, e.g., Derven, 2014), the removal of barriers for participating in various occupations—such as women's entry to male-dominated fields and vice versa—and the introduction of inclusive procurement practices (EBRD, 2017).

A core category of urban value creation is *entrepreneurship and financial inclusion* by offering tailored financial and business advisory services. Micro-finance and other financial instruments and support services can be offered to those who face disproportionate barriers to accessing the formal financial system and wider business ecosystem. In an alternative approach, solutions are designed that fit specific phases of the business cycle, from business incubation and start-upping to economic gardening. An additional set of actions goes beyond conventional business support toward self-employment, social entrepreneurship, and the civic economy (cf.

Greenwood & Holt, 2015). Special inclusive measures may range from bringing together finance and skill development to business advice to support senior, youth, women, and ethnic entrepreneurship (EBRD, 2017; Ibrahim & Galt, 2011; Isele & Rogoff, 2014; Yadav & Unni, 2016).

Access to services that enhance economic opportunities implies a focus on fostering economic inclusion by supporting access to improved transport and connectivity as well as to services that enhance the economic opportunities of targeted segments of the population. Actions include increasing connectivity through transport services, road infrastructure that substantially enhances access to jobs, markets, education, and health care of population in underserved areas, and enhancing access to digital connectivity to create or substantially improve access to markets, jobs, and resources (EBRD, 2017).

Any of the abovementioned policy choices and solutions requires keen awareness of governance arrangements in which they should be embedded. That will be the topic of Chap. 6.

References

Adams, M., & Bell, L. (Eds.). (2016). *Teaching for Diversity and Social Justice* (3rd ed.). New York: Routledge.

ADB. (2017). *Enabling Inclusive Cities: Tool Kit for Inclusive Urban Development.* Mandaluyong City, Philippines: Asian Development Bank. Retrieved July 16, 2020, from https://www.adb.org/sites/default/files/institutional-document/223096/enabling-inclusive-cities.pdf

Berube, A., Bosland, J., Greene, S., & Rush, C. (2018). Building Shared Prosperity in America's Cities. Shared Prosperity Partnership. Retrieved July 17, 2020, from https://www.brookings.edu/wp-content/uploads/2018/06/ACP1039-SP2-Framing-Paper-Final.pdf

Bills, A., Armstrong, D., & Howard, N. (2020). Scaled-up 'safety-net' Schooling and the 'wicked problem' of Educational Exclusion in South Australia: Problem or Solution? *The Australian Educational Researcher, 47*, 239–261. https://doi.org/10.1007/s13384-019-00353-z

Crenshaw, K. (1989). Demarginalizing the Intersection of Race and Sex: A Black Feminist Critique of Antidiscrimination Doctrine, Feminist Theory and Antiracist Politics. *University of Chicago Legal Forum, 1989* (1), Article 8. Retrieved from http://chicagounbound.uchicago.edu/uclf/vol1989/iss1/8

Cyrus, K. (2017). Multiple Minorities as Multiply Marginalized: Applying the Minority Stress Theory to LGBTQ People of Color. *Journal of Gay & Lesbian Mental Health, 21*(3), 194–202. https://doi.org/10.1080/19359705.2017.1320739

Derven, M. (2014). Diversity and Inclusion by Design: best Practices from Six Global Companies. *Industrial and Commercial Training, 46*(2), 84–91.

EBRD. (2017). Economic Inclusion Strategy (EIS) 2017–2021. European Bank for Reconstruction and Development. Retrieved July 13, 2020, from https://www.ebrd.com/ebrd-economic-inclusion-strategy.pdf

Fukuyama, F. (1992). *The End of History and the Last Man*. New York: The Free Press.

Furedi, F. (2019, March 1). A Perpetual War of Identities. *Spiked*. Retrieved July 11, 2020, from https://www.spiked-online.com/2019/03/01/a-perpetual-war-of-identities/

Greenwood, D. T., & Holt, R. P. F. (2015). *Local Economic Development in the 21st Century: Quality of Live and Sustainability*. London and New York: Routledge.

Haidt, J. (2017, December 17). The Age of Outrage: What the Current Political Climate is Doing to Our Country and Our Universities. *City Journal*. Manhattan Institute for Policy Research. Retrieved July 11, 2020, from https://www.city-journal.org/html/age-outrage-15608.html

Haidt, J., & Rose-Stockwell, T. (2019, December). The Dark Psychology of Social Networks: Why it Feels Like Everything Is Going Haywire. *The Atlantic*. Retrieved July 11, 2020, from https://www.theatlantic.com/magazine/archive/2019/12/social-media-democracy/600763/

Hambleton, R. (2015). *Leading the Inclusive City: Place-based Innovation for a Bounded Planet*. Bristol, UK: Policy Press.

Ibrahim, G., & Galt, V. (2011). Explaining Ethnic Entrepreneurship: An Evolutionary Economics Approach. *International Business Review, 20*(6), 607–613. https://doi.org/10.1016/j.ibusrev.2011.02.010

Isele, E., & Rogoff, E. G. (2014). Senior Entrepreneurship: The New Normal. *Public Policy & Aging Report, 24*, 141–147. https://doi.org/10.1093/ppar/pru043

Jacobs, M., & Mazzucato, M. (Eds.). (2016). *Rethinking Capitalism: Economics and Policy for Sustainable and Inclusive Growth*. Chichester, UK: Wiley-Blackwell.

Lee, N. (2019). Inclusive Growth in Cities: A Sympathetic Critique. *Regional Studies, 53*(3), 424–434. https://doi.org/10.1080/00343404.2018.1476753

Michie, S., van Stralen, M. M., & West, R. (2011). The Behaviour Change Wheel: A New Method for Characterising and Designing Behaviour Change Interventions. *Implementation Science, 6*, article 42. https://doi.org/10.1186/1748-5908-6-42

Mouffe, C. (2005). *On the Political*. Abingdon and New York: Routledge.

Naidu, S., Rodrik, D., & Zucman, G. (2019, January). Economics for Inclusive Prosperity: An Introduction. *EfIP Research Brief*. Economists for Inclusive Prosperity. Retrieved October 31, 2019, from https://econfip.org/wp-content/uploads/2019/02/1.Economics-for-Inclusive-Prosperity-An-Introduction.pdf

OECD. (2015). *Government at a Glance 2015*. Paris: OECD Publishing. https://doi.org/10.1787/gov_glance-2015-en

Smith, C. E. (2019, September 12). Here's How We Can Design Inclusive Cities. *World Economic Forum*. Retrieved July 12, 2020, from https://www.weforum.org/agenda/2019/09/here-s-how-we-can-design-inclusive-cities/

Smyth, J. (2010). Speaking Back to Educational Policy: Why Social Inclusion Will Not Work for Disadvantaged Australian Schools. *Critical Studies in Education*, *51*(2), 113–128. https://doi.org/10.1080/17508481003742320

Stilwell, C. (2016). Public Libraries and Social Inclusion: An Update from South Africa. In U. Gorham, N. G. Taylor, & P. T. Jaeger (Eds.), *Perspectives on Libraries as Institutions of Human Rights and Social Justice* (Advances in Librarianship) (Vol. 41, pp. 119–146). Emerald Group Publishing Limited. https://doi.org/10.1108/S0065-283020160000041006

Yadav, V., & Unni, J. (2016). Women Entrepreneurship: Research Review and Future Directions. *Journal of Global Entrepreneurship Research, 6*, article 12. https://doi.org/10.1186/s40497-016-0055-x

Governing the Inclusive City

Abstract Building the inclusive city calls for collaborative and synergistic creation of shared prosperity, which in turn is deemed to require efforts of all segments of the urban population. Sufficient governance arrangements must allow for this. Local government is only one player in this complex setting. Chapter 6 pinpoints and positions various types of organizations whose resources and support are needed for inclusive urban development. These include large multinational corporations, locally embedded start-ups and entrepreneurs, NGOs and social entrepreneurs, and local residents. The most typical modes of governance in which they cooperate are partnerships, networks, and platforms. In many cases, anchor institutions, such as universities and hospitals, can play essential roles because of their strong leverage and connection to local community.

Keywords Stakeholder • Governance • Co-creation • Mode of governance • Shared prosperity • Anchor institution

A Stakeholder-Oriented Approach

To fulfill the promise of building an inclusive city, the role of various local stakeholders in promoting social inclusion and their potential to directly or indirectly support inclusion-driven value creation is to be identified. This insight boils down to how the making of an inclusive city needs to be structured in terms of governance and stakeholder engagement.

© The Author(s) 2020
A.-V. Anttiroiko, M. de Jong, *The Inclusive City*,
https://doi.org/10.1007/978-3-030-61365-5_6

This chapter discusses institutional arrangements conducive to economic inclusion. It goes without saying that local government cannot promote inclusive growth and shared prosperity on its own. This challenge requires, first of all, that many or all key stakeholders of the city are involved and, secondly, that relevant local, national, and at times also international institutional organizations and resources are tuned in to support such a critical urban transformation.

When attempting to involve local actors in *collaborative and synergistic value creation*, command-and-control style management is unlikely to bear fruit. The primary governance mechanism cannot be markets either, due to the relational and multidimensional nature and the essential social dimension of the interaction and negotiation patterns this policy challenge implies. Rather, inclusion-oriented development must primarily be built on the forms of collaborative and distributive governance, which allow equal, flexible, mutually beneficial, and dynamically adjustable relations between actors involved in local public affairs. Although this style is often proclaimed in words, actual application in daily practice still lags behind among many local governments.

It is important to emphasize here that economic inclusion should be partly fully open and inclusive, partly selective and targeted. The other critical point is that the shift in perspective from citizens' political rights to stakeholders' value creation implies that the concepts developed within the participatory turn in democratic theory and practice must be refined: participation should be approached as value co-creation with a special interest in how public governance can help local stakeholders climb higher on the ladder of value creation.

Tensional Road to Inclusion

Creating an inclusive city should amount to setting up a win-win scheme socially, politically, and economically. It is socially desirable because inclusion motivated by social ethics tends to increase social justice, equality, cohesion, and a sharing mentality in society. It is politically justified due to a widening of opportunities for political participation and influence among stakeholders. It is economically beneficial as it improves the utilization of the resources in the community through inclusive practices of established businesses, start-uppers, social entrepreneurs, and civil society. But it does create societal tensions too.

To start with, there are no policies without opportunity costs, no new public services without initial lack or stringency of resourcing, and no new actions without someone's extra efforts or sacrifice being required. As inclusion opens new channels to various groups, it reshapes social relations and dynamics and may occasionally create side-effects and tensions. For example, over time providing support to the poor tends to increase welfare dependency among recipient groups, and similarly growing up with parents on welfare benefits increases the likelihood of becoming welfare recipient at later stages in life (Edmark & Hanspers, 2015). Another example is race- and region-conscious admission policies applied by some prestigious universities in the USA and in China, which give students from ethnic minorities or underdeveloped regions advantages in getting into college (e.g., Reilly, 2019). Such policies are likely to evoke resentment among groups, which do not enjoy such privileges or are even put at a disadvantage.

Similarly, conflicts may arise dynamically because of values and viewpoints of people involved, as has been the case with immigration policies in many European countries in the mid-2015, in which initially tolerant people began filibustering after the dramatic local impact of the influx of immigrants from the Middle East and Africa in their towns and cities became palpable (e.g., Bershidsky, 2018). This happened even in Denmark and Sweden, otherwise known as among the most tolerant and inclusive societies in the world. Interestingly, in some cities ethnic groups that once were marginalized minorities have grown large and influential, as in the case of Miami (FL), with some 72% being Latinos and another 15% African Americans, while non-Hispanic white residents make up only 10% of urban population. The "white flight" and immigration have affected practically every aspect of everyday life in the city. Lastly, an example characteristic of our time is the demand for equal rights made by the LGBTQI community which promotes not only its self-affirmation and societal mainstreaming but incurs increasingly active resistance from conservatives and orthodox religious segments of society.

When considering the above issues from an economic point of view, this discussion acquires additional nuance, since we can easily find cases showing that in retrospect positive discrimination turned out to be justified and that *migration* has had a positive impact on many economies (Bodvarsson & van den Berg, 2013). Similarly, *tolerance* is assumed to be one of the building blocks for creative city-oriented economic development, and *LGBTQI inclusion* correlates positively with economic growth

(Badgett, Park, & Flores, 2018). In the US context, it was found that *diversity* increases wages in both high- and low-income groups (Kemeny, Cooke, & Marek Zeitlin, 2017). Given that the inclusion agenda driven by identity politics is easily prone to ideological bias in Western democracies and elsewhere, it is worth considering these economic benefits and applying transparency, honesty, and evidence-based premises when assessing, communicating, and building the inclusive city agenda.

GOVERNANCE ARRANGEMENTS FOR SHARED URBAN PROSPERITY

Local government is a legitimate instance of the democratically organized system that produces authoritative decisions on local public affairs. Beside this political-administrative core, local authorities apply new forms of organization, persuasive strategies, and multi-sectoral approaches in order to involve local stakeholders in the promotion of local development. Such activities fall under the concept of *public governance*, which is about the coordination and use of various forms of institutional arrangements for involving stakeholders and orchestrating multi-sectoral relations in policy-making and implementation in the pursuit of collective interest. This brings new public governance close to stakeholder management (Rixon, 2010).

There are a few specific discourses in which *inclusive governance* has been explicitly discussed. One of them is the debate on international development cooperation, within which experts have concluded that improved governance leads to better development outcomes (Hickey, Sen, & Bukenya, 2015). Another area in which inclusive governance has been explicitly discussed is neighborhood development and urban regeneration, which generally aim at social cohesion, creative solutions to urban development, and resident engagement (Cabeza, Eizaguirre, & Pradel, 2015; Cook & Swyngedouw, 2012). A third area is inclusion in internal governance of institutions, organizations, and workplaces (e.g., Dobusch, 2014). At the organizational level, inclusion refers to specific structurally and culturally embedded aspects of signification, domination, and legitimation on which organizational actors draw to produce and reproduce inclusionary behavior. In the business context, such a Diversity and Inclusion framework is most commonly applied to recruitment, training, and informal gatherings (Ortlieb & Sieben, 2014).

Previously mentioned international development organizations have been influential in setting this agenda by demanding better inclusion and representation as their priorities in international cooperation. The United Nations' *Sustainable Development Goals* (SDGs) are the high-level political articulations of such a view, promoting inclusive economic growth (Goal 8), inclusive and sustainable industrialization (Goal 9), inclusive, safe, resilient, and sustainable development of urban settlements (Goal 11), and building effective, accountable, and inclusive institutions at all levels (Goal 16) (see at https://sustainabledevelopment.un.org/sdgs). These amount to an ambitious global agenda.

To give another example, the London Declaration on Inclusive Governance for a Renewed Commonwealth sets similar kind of agenda for inclusion:

> Building inclusive, transparent and accountable governance, institutions and decision-making processes, that include all marginalised communities and individuals in decision-making and adherence to the Commonwealth Charter, with its strong emphasis on human rights, are crucial building blocks for Commonwealth inclusion. Ending exclusion also necessitates greater accountability, legislative reform, honesty and transparent governance. (CPF, 2018)

Development cooperation-oriented inclusive governance aims at supporting marginalized groups and providing them access to participate effectively in mainstream economic, political, and social systems. If assessed only from this point of view, inclusive governance reflects the primary aspects of social inclusion as presented in the UN agenda. It includes citizen participation, fairness, respect for human rights, empowering marginalized groups, an inclusive political culture, and good governance. In this discourse, inclusiveness boils down to the empowerment of the poor, the participation of civil society, and the strengthening of responsive and accountable institutions (World Bank, 2005). It closely resembles a social view of good governance, which promotes the establishment of effective, accountable, and inclusive institutions and governance processes.

Fostering inclusion is a process in which politics, history, formal and informal institutions, agency, and socio-economic and political structures matter (see Hickey et al., 2015). Moreover, Rocha Menocal and others (2019) remind us that an important lesson learned from history is that numerous good intentions and policy goals do not necessarily go together well or have mutually reinforcing effects. There are inherent tensions and trade-offs between different processes of transformation and priorities for fostering inclusive societies. Moreover, inclusion may occasionally be asymmetric due to differences in local actors' orientations, capacities, and resources; this obviously presents challenges to urban governance.

STAKEHOLDERS IN ECONOMIC INCLUSION

Economic inclusion entails that creating wealth and sharing it widely within an urban community are both essential; principles of governance must reflect this endeavor. First and foremost, from an economic point of view it should empower practically all actors in the local community, for they all possess some potential and show some capacity to contribute to local value creation. Socially speaking, local governments should utilize special participatory tools to give underrepresented and marginalized groups a voice, show appreciation of their involvement, demonstrate the value of their participation, and reward them for their efforts and achievements. The above two components jointly are fruitful soil for broad-based citizen and stakeholder engagement in value creation.

The other side of the picture is to target primal value creators, in which talent pool, technological expertise, businesses, and anchor institutions are of critical importance. Governance for shared prosperity has to be sensitive to essential differences among economic actors—multinationals, established corporations, SMEs, entrepreneurs, start-ups, and socially oriented organizations—since these differences require them to be treated differently and receive a different emphasis in governance arrangements. These distinctions in the governance setting are illustrated in Fig. 6.1.

First, a high-value strategy for inclusion is built on mainstream businesses' *Diversity and Inclusion* (D&I) concept, which refers to actions, programs, and company-wide policies that encourage representation and participation of diverse groups of people—most notably gender, ethnicity, culture, ableness, and age—in the key activities throughout the organization (see, e.g., Derven, 2014). This approach gains its justification from the empirical fact that companies with greater national, cultural, and gender diversity at the senior level show better business performance. Inclusive leadership and organization culture outperform their less diverse competitors (Hunt, Prince, Dixon-Fyle, & Yee, 2018). Inclusive organizations also tend to be better in retaining their skilled and talented employees. This aspect is becoming critical in the innovation-driven competitive

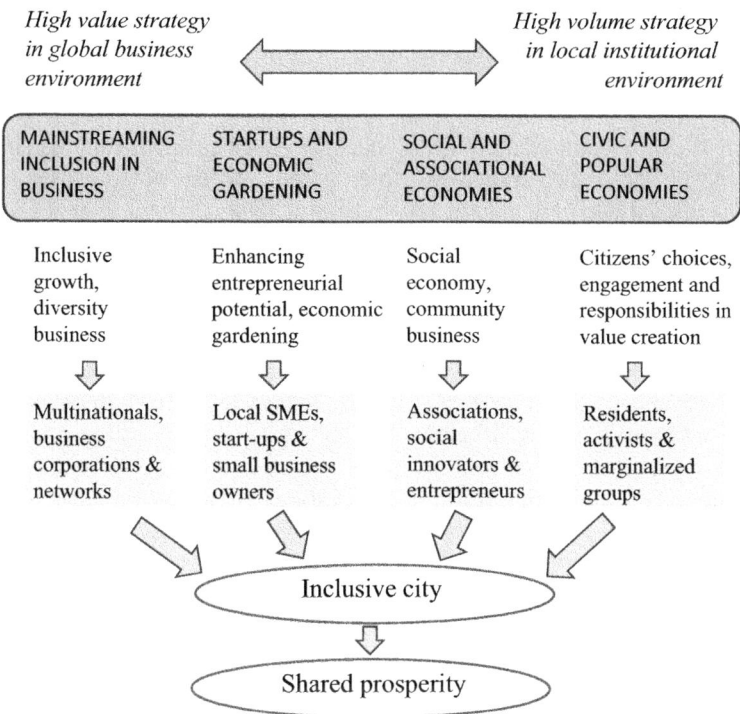

High value strategy in global business environment ⟷ *High volume strategy in local institutional environment*

MAINSTREAMING INCLUSION IN BUSINESS	STARTUPS AND ECONOMIC GARDENING	SOCIAL AND ASSOCIATIONAL ECONOMIES	CIVIC AND POPULAR ECONOMIES
Inclusive growth, diversity business	Enhancing entrepreneurial potential, economic gardening	Social economy, community business	Citizens' choices, engagement and responsibilities in value creation
Multinationals, business corporations & networks	Local SMEs, start-ups & small business owners	Associations, social innovators & entrepreneurs	Residents, activists & marginalized groups

Inclusive city

Shared prosperity

Fig. 6.1 Key stakeholders in economic inclusion policy

global environment and global competition for talent, which further emphasizes the appeal of diverse and tolerant workplaces (Gundling, Caldwell, & Cvitkovich, 2015). Moreover, D&I strategies and capabilities create preconditions for business intelligence, creativity, and novelty in action. Moreover, in the global markets it is diversity that helps companies to reflect the diversity of their future growth markets (see, e.g., Donovan & Kaplan, 2019).

Second, scale and approach change when we focus on *inclusive entrepreneurship, self-employment, business incubation, start-upping, and economic gardening*. This can be about solopreneurship or starting a micro or small business, which requires determination and a sufficient variety of competences that enable people to turn their ideas into profitable business. At the advanced level we speak of economic gardening, which focuses on growth-oriented firms or so-called second-stagers—with some 10–99 employees and at least some 1 million USD in revenues—for they produce the greatest economic impact on localities as they are big enough to bring money into the community from outside markets, yet are usually still firmly local. In industrial policy, such a focus implies nurturing local businesses rather than attracting "big game" from outside the area (Gibbons, 2010).

A third type of stakeholders in economic life is connected with previously mentioned inclusive entrepreneurship but has an explicit social and community orientation, as seen in socially oriented self-employment, community businesses, and so-called *social economy organizations* (SEOs), which do business in various organizational forms—cooperatives, mutuals, charities, and social businesses—driven by a social mission and commitment to community well-being. This category includes all socially oriented for-profit enterprises, on the one hand, and social enterprises, non-governmental organizations (NGOs) and associations that create value for their community, on the other (see Cooke & Morgan, 1998; Gonzales, 2007; Colenbrander, et al., 2017).

Fourth, the last broad category to be discussed here is the *civic economy*, which brings the economic activities of civil society under the spotlight. It is shaped by new technologies, novel forms of social organization, and adoption of forward-looking principles, such as openness and sharing. It is in some occasions characterized as fusing the culture of Web 2.0 with civic purpose. As an industrial or economic development policy agenda, it has been referred to as people-centered economic development (Greenwood & Holt, 2010). Civic economy implies that citizens share, collaborate, and co-create in order to tackle local and social challenges and utilize emerging opportunities. Some of these activities may fall into self-employment or social entrepreneurship, having thus intersecting areas with the social economy and early stage entrepreneurship. As a whole, however, these civic activities form a broad category that cannot be meaningfully reduced to conventional institutionalized aspects of economic life. The civic economy is becoming a social, entrepreneurial, and financial power. It is an essential aspect of the platform and network economies as well as the rising "fourth pillar" in the Quadruple Helix (industry, government, academia, and users/civil society) as it supplements its traditional role as user and target of value-adding activities of other helixes by its productive and value creation functions (EUKN, 2015; Hasche, Höglund, & Linton, 2019).

FROM PARTICIPATION TO CO-CREATION
AND VALUE ENHANCEMENT

Modern public governance builds on democratic institutions and structures. When we zoom in on this scene, one factor appears as fundamental building block for genuine social and political inclusion, *citizen participation* (see Baum, 2015; on benefits and limits of participatory and inclusive governance, see Richter, 2018). It is a manifestation of inclusion through active agency and citizen-centric governance. That said, it is also noteworthy that inclusiveness can become asymmetric or biased because of differences in people's interests, capacities, and resources. That is why there is a need to pay attention to two local groups in particular: (a) those who bear a lot of value creation potential, and (b) those who are marginalized and less likely to be able to participate in and contribute to mainstream society without special support and encouragement. The inclusive city aims to ensure that chances for meaningful and feasible inclusion are maximized for both groups.

Governing for shared prosperity requires that the entire urban paradigm is switched from closed to open. Goldsmith and Kleiman (2017) argue that this entails a few *critical transformations*, including transition (a) from vertical governance with an associated local information monopoly to a platform provider of networked and enabled solutions; (b) from government organized for its own convenience, professionalism and administrative logic to one that puts the citizen and key value creators at the center; and (c) from the primary producer of public value to an integrator of resources and contributions from a wide swath of external entities.

Another requirement brought in by a diversity of stakeholders is the need for sufficient variation in *forms, methods, and scales of urban public governance*. This means that "one size fits all" thinking should give way to target group-sensitive solutions, flexibility, and hybrid and mixed governance arrangements, which have social and economic inclusion as their overall framework and inclusive growth and shared prosperity as their generic goal.

There is a wide range of *mechanisms and forms of stakeholder engagement*, often categorized on the basis of the degree to which they allow citizen control. A fundamental distinction can be made between non-participation (e.g., information sharing), participation, and direct citizen control, based on Arnstein's (1969) classic paper about the ladder of citizen participation and Lee, Loutas, Sánchez-Nielsen, Mogulkoc, and Lacigova's (2011) Inform-Consult-Empower scheme. Our focus here is slightly different, though, for rather than the degree of citizen influence or control or the intensity or transformational power of citizen participation, our interest lies in finding the best possible ways to involve local actors in entrepreneurship, value generation, co-creation, and sharing. One way of systematizing the levels of value creation is illustrated in Fig. 6.2. It describes value creation development from attitudinal change and capacity building toward different levels of genuine organized value creation ranging from facilitated action to value orchestration, ending with "leading for value," which revolves around insightful leadership in complex global business environment to guide high value-adding producers in delivering value for their customers. At the lower rungs of the ladder, the emphasis is on grassroots-level bustle, high volumes, synergies of the crowd, and local sources of vitality, while on the highest-level focus is on high

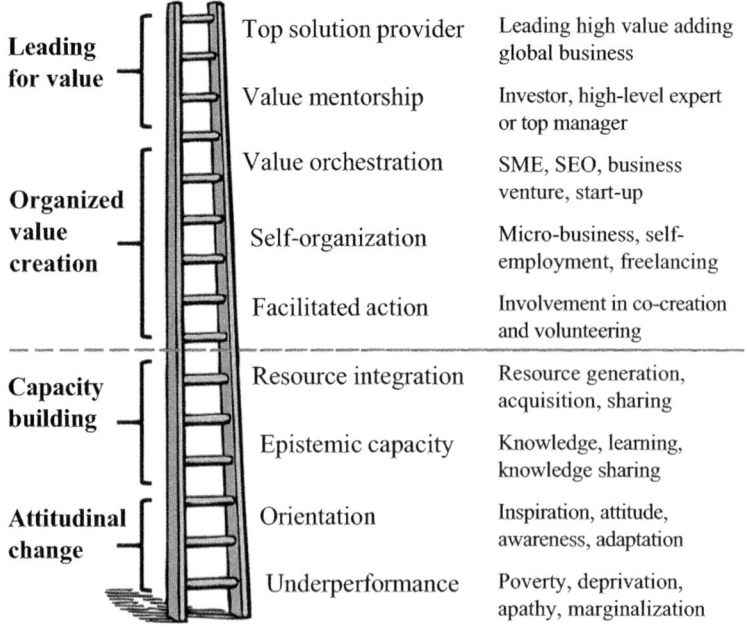

Fig. 6.2 The ladder of stakeholder value creation

value-added activities of key players in a complex technological-economic environment.

To concretize the picture of governance for economic inclusion, we will next discuss *partnerships* with anchor institutions and large business organizations, *networking* with a larger pool of institutional actors that form a cluster or service ecosystem, and *platforms* and other engagement mechanisms that match businesses with citizens and gather wider audiences in value creation. These three forms of heterarchical governance are illustrated in Table 6.1.

Table 6.1 Three modes of governance for economic inclusion

	Partnerships	*Networks*	*Platforms*
Primary target groups	Anchor institutions, established corporations, large SEOs	Small and medium-sized enterprises (SMEs), social economy organizations (SEOs), start-uppers, self-employed	Citizens, customers, disadvantaged groups, marginalized minorities, different age groups
Paradigmatic relation	Partnership with an anchor institution	Local development network	Participatory innovation platform
Theoretical foundation	Economic inclusion, corporate social responsibility, diversity, public-private partnership (PPP)	Entrepreneurial society, start-up city, social and solidarity economy (SSE), network governance	Participatory democracy, urban commons, transformational politics, sharing city, platform governance, ecosystem thinking
Strategic focus	Mainstreaming diversity and inclusion, reaching out to communities	Resource pooling, sharing, cross-sector collaboration	User experience, capacity building, co-production, empowerment, utilization of connections
Added value	Business performance, return on investment (ROI)	Collaborative synergies and business opportunities, network effect	Knowledge and learning, diversity, grassroots business
Mechanisms and governance activities	Raising awareness, meetings and events, contracts	Networking, recognition of champions, mentoring	Training, co-creation platforms, advice for starting a business

THE ROLE OF ANCHOR INSTITUTIONS

Anchor institutions are immobile, place-based public, non-profit, or for-profit organizations, which assume an institutional governing role as their impact on community becomes significant and, reversely, the development of the surrounding community becomes important to them. This entails that such an institution moves beyond its core business by showing social responsibility, committing itself to community engagement, and initiating actions that help the host community thrive. We may group such institutions into three types: (a) established businesses, (b) knowledge, service, and cultural institutions, and (c) social economy organizations.

First, when discussing established businesses as a subcategory of anchor institutions, we refer to a group of large, resourceful, and economically successful institutions, such as big corporations, high-tech companies, and real estate developers (Florida & Pedigo, 2017). They usually have a stake in urban development, especially if they take corporate social responsibility seriously and are willing to commit themselves to involving the corporate community, which provides opportunities for the development of partnerships between proactive corporations, local government, and associations (van den Berg, Braun, & Otgaar, 2004).

Florida (2015) claims that globalization has hit hard at many once-thriving manufacturers and large corporations as well as the cities that once housed them. There has been a gradual shift from such industrial giants to clusters of companies, talent, and support industries, which themselves often have close relationships with research universities, medical centers, and other creative or knowledge-based institutions. Gradually the same role has been assumed by wellness and hospitality facilities, such as large spas and convention centers, as well as large utilities and logistic hubs. In short, partnering for inclusive growth and shared prosperity calls for anchor institutions to combine their considerable resources to support diversity and equity in local communities (Florida, Pedigo, & Bendix, 2018; see also Florida & Pedigo, 2017; Florida & McLean, 2017).

Second, a special category of primarily non-profit anchor institutions includes large universities, hospitals, and medical centers, sometimes referred to as "meds and eds," and cultural facilities, such as big theaters and concert halls. They are often urban landmarks with strong local roots, some of them being among the largest employers in their communities with high impact on local economy through employment and purchasing power. One of the primary institutions in this respect is the *university*, which can serve as a place-based catalyst for urban change (Perry, Wiewel, & Menendez, 2009). Their roles vary depending on the profile of the institution and the special features of the city. The utilization of academic research requires the use of means that are tailored to the innovation needs of the city. Rather than through a fashionable technology transfer model, such an impact materializes best in the form of education and the provision of discussion forums on technological and social trends (Lester, 2007). Another important anchor institution is the *hospital.* Hospitals contribute to local development by supplementing their traditional focus on the provision of direct patient care by using mechanisms to address the social determinants of health in local communities (Franz, Skinner, Wynn, & Kelleher, 2019).

Third, the more the locality hosts SEOs and NGOs, the more likely it is that it can generate institutional thickness, utilize locally unique assets, and find niches in the social economy. The involvement of the Social and Solidarity Economy (SSE) is of vital importance from the perspective of urban inclusive prosperity; city governments may well benefit from giving SEOs an explicit role in strategic economic plans as well as in relevant decision-making structures of local government or local development agencies (Vickers, Westall, Spear, Brennan, & Syrett, 2017).

Representatives and business intermediaries in SEOs and NGOs have special capacities in performing and encouraging cross-sector collaboration and networking for knowledge-sharing and action around priority challenges. Local governments benefit from supporting local community-anchored SEOs—such as housing associations or community businesses—to catalyze collaboration across the social economy to improve job creation, community pride, and well-being in deprived local areas. Social economy intermediaries can play a key role in exchanging good practices and ideas, including the use of technology, applying approaches to developing a collaborative economy, or in case of larger established SEOs, providing support to smaller SEOs and start-ups. Such partnerships could be expanded by bringing SEOs together with other institutional actors, most notably Triple Helix institutions (business, government, universities) and occasionally even trade unions and civic associations that represent special areas of the social economy (Vickers et al., 2017).

Networking for Inclusive Growth

Traditional public administration began to change gradually in the post-war years, first through marketization associated with New Public Management and later with the utilization of partnerships, networks, and other forms of non-hierarchical governance structures. The emergence of the latter is sometimes referred to as network, associative, distributed, or collaborative governance, emphasizing trust, reciprocity, learning, and empowerment as main preconditions for successful joint action. *Networks* are collaborative arrangements that facilitate the pooling of network members' resources for the attainment of shared goals (Bovaird, Löffler, & Parrado-Díez, 2002). In our context, network management aims at coordinating the interests and strategies of different stakeholders within a generic policy goal of enhancing inclusive growth and shared prosperity.

Networks are an important means for exchanging knowledge and utilizing the pool of resources owned by different actors and groups in society. When local players work through an integrated and networked approach, they are better equipped to work on development processes and to make them more effective, inclusive, and transparent. There is empirical evidence of the increased importance of forming networks in the pursuit of inclusive prosperity (UNIDO, 2013).

The dynamic core of network governance is that it enables small-scale providers to join their efforts, pool resources, share risks, and thus create offerings that they would have not been able to make independently. Many local and national networks and partnerships promote the inclusive economy, such as local innovation networks, Local Strategic Partnerships (LSPs) in nearly all local government jurisdictions in England to facilitate inter-sectoral cooperation, or a network of Silver Human Resource Centers in Japan that provide work opportunities for older people. As examples of macro-regional networks that work on social and economic inclusion, we wish to mention the Network for Inclusive Cities in Europe (NICE), the European Network for Rural Development, and the European Network of Innovation for Inclusion. In the area of global economic inclusion, beside UN-based networks we could mention the Network for Open Economies and Inclusive Societies (NOEIS), which is committed to advancing a well-functioning open global economy while reducing excessive inequalities (see, e.g., Antonelli, 2013; Shafique, Antink, Clay, & Cox, 2019).

THE ROLE OF URBAN AND DIGITAL PLATFORMS

We have previously discussed anchor institutions and networks, which focus on institutional actors known to have the disposal of resources and capabilities needed in the promotion of local economic development. In the inclusive city, even if the assumed added value of an individual citizen may not be that significant, such contributions accumulate, create synergies, inspire, and have dynamic impacts *en masse*. Such added value emerges in two primary forms. First, stakeholder engagement can facilitate participation and influence policy decisions, increasing the likelihood of policy outcomes that deliver for the many, not just the few (OECD, 2015). On the other hand, broad-based stakeholder involvement transforms into actions and interactions that generate value considerably exceeding the resources that local governments alone can allocate to inclusionary programs and related policy measures. We are not only dealing with participation in a political sense, but also in an economic sense of the term, thus referring to everyone's ability to participate in society as a value creator.

It is genuinely difficult to match economic development with broad-based stakeholder, community, and citizen participation. In such challenging policy environments, discourse may easily become expert-driven, and top-down partnership structures begin to legitimate policy decisions taken by local elites often influenced by extra-local authorities or expert organizations (cf. Raco, 2000). Meeting the challenge of building genuinely inclusive processes that bring added value to the community requires, first, that the appropriate range of interests is engaged in the process, including those normally excluded from decision-making by institutionalized inequities (Bryson, Quick, Slotterback, & Crosby, 2013), and second, that the opportunities for learning, synergies, and value creation, including business opportunity enhancement, are identified and utilized in properly facilitated processes. Such actions should be made an integral part of local economic development policy (Greenwood & Holt, 2010).

Platforms are a fairly recently emerged organizational form that has spread from innovation-oriented governance to other areas of urban governance. Platforms epitomize the idea that urban governments can in many cases pursue public interest simply by letting community members organize themselves and create value or rely on decentralized solutions that at the aggregate level generate public value (Bollier, 2016). The importance of platforms derives from their basic features as dynamic digital or hybrid structures that gather relevant actors on a voluntary basis to co-create value through quantities, connections, or new content. There are various kinds of *digital participatory platforms* (DPPs) in the making in different parts of the world, with an idea of supporting open citizen participation (see Falco & Kleinhans, 2018). Basic functions of DPPs are illustrated in Table 6.2.

An illuminating example of local innovation platform is Demola in Tampere, Finland, which utilizes the potential of local university students by matching them with local businesses and other organizations. As examples of digital platforms that facilitate communication and interaction at the neighborhood level, we may mention Nextdoor and Front Porch Forum. Some of these platforms are genuinely open, decentralized, and empowering, such as Helsinki Region Infoshare (HRI). It is a digital platform that provides data sets of municipalities in the Greater Helsinki area, which everyone can freely use (Anttiroiko, 2016). There are also a few digital platforms that focus on techno-economic inclusion. One of them is Mindtree.Org, a corporate social responsibility (CSR) initiative of the IT and outsourcing company Mindtree. The idea is to build an inclusive society through digital platforms that help to democratize technology for micro-entrepreneurs (see https://www.mindtree.org/).

Another category of platforms has its root in sharing economy (eBay, Airbnb, Uber, Campspace, Freelancer, etc.), which is actually directly associated with economic inclusion. Some studies tentatively show that in developing countries, platforms in the sharing economy in general strengthen trust, confidence, and empowerment. A good example is the inclusion of unemployed groups through self-employment or micro-entrepreneurship. The exclusionary elements that hold development back to a degree include gender bias, gender/age issues, and problems with access due to unfavorable geographic locations (Malik & Wahaj, 2019).

It is likely that in the increasingly globalized and techno-savvy environments the digital platforms will have a greater role in including people in value creation. This requires, however, a sufficiently high level of digital and media literacy in order to empower people to interact with local and extra-local value processes and related business ecosystems.

References

Antonelli, G. (2013). The Local Innovation Networks: An Explorative Study of Success Cluster. *The Business Review*, Cambridge, *21*(2), 205–211.

Table 6.2   Platforms at different levels of citizen-government relationships

Levels	Description	Examples of platforms
Information sharing	One-way communication (broadcasting) from government to citizens.	Civic Insight (SA) OS City (Netherlands) Tell Us Toolkit (UK)
Consulting and reporting	One-way communication from citizens to governments	Emotional maps (Czech Rep.) MySidewalk (USA) PlaceSpeak (UK)
Interaction	Two-way communication with dialogue and feedback between citizens and government representatives	Civocracy (Germany) Ethelo (Canada) Granicus (USA) OpenDCN (Italy) SpeakUpAustin (USA) FixMyStreet (UK) WhatDoTheyKnow (UK)
Co-production	The public sector and citizens making better use of each other's assets and resources to achieve better outcomes and improved efficiency	MetroQuest (USA) Carticipe/Debatomap (France) Crowdbrite (USA) CityLab010 (Netherlands) Maptionnaire (Finland) TransformCity (Netherlands) Urban Interactive Studio (USA)
Self-organization (public matters)	Citizens create solutions independently that are to be recognized, facilitated, or adopted by governments and require some government action	BUURbook (Netherlands) Airesis (Italy) FragNebenan (Austria) Front Porch Forum (USA)

Source: Adopted from Falco and Kleinhans (2018)

Anttiroiko, A.-V. (2016). City-as-a-Platform: The Rise of Participatory Innovation Platforms in Finnish Cities. *Sustainability, 8*(9), article 922. Retrieved from https://www.mdpi.com/2071-1050/8/9/922

Arnstein, S. R. (1969). A Ladder of Citizen Participation. *Journal of the American Institute of Planners, 35*(4), 216–224.

Badgett, M. V. L., Park, A., & Flores, A. (2018, March). Links between Economic Development and New Measures of LGBT Inclusion. *The Williams Institute*, UCLA School of Law. Retrieved November 21, 2019, from https://williaminstitute.law.ucla.edu/wp-content/uploads/GDP-and-LGBT-Inclusion-April-2018.pdf

Baum, H. S. (2015). Citizen Participation. In J. D. Wright (Ed.), *International Encyclopedia of the Social & Behavioral Sciences* (2nd ed., pp. 625–630). Oxford: Elsevier.

Bershidsky, L. (2018, December 1). Sweden's Decades-Long Failure to Integrate. *Bloomberg Opinion*. Retrieved November 19, 2019, from https://www.bloomberg.com/opinion/articles/2018-12-01/sweden-s-anti-immigration-wave-is-based-on-a-failure-to-integrate

Bodvarsson, Ö. B., & van den Berg, H. (2013). *The Economics of Immigration: Theory and Policy*. New York; Heidelberg: Springer.

Bollier, D. (2016). *The City as Platform: How Digital Networks Are Changing Urban Life and Governance*. Washington, DC: The Aspen Institute.

Bovaird, T., Löffler, E., & Parrado-Díez, S. (2002). *Developing Local Governance Networks in Europe*. Baden-Baden: Nomos Verlagsgesellschaft.

Bryson, J., Quick, K., Slotterback, C., & Crosby, B. (2013). Designing Public Participation Processes. *Public Administration Review, 73*(1), 23–34.

Cabeza, M., Eizaguirre, S., & Pradel, M. (2015). Social Innovation and Creativity in Cities: A Socially Inclusive Governance Approach in Two Peripheral Spaces of Barcelona. *City, Culture and Society, 6*(4), 93–100.

Colenbrander, A., Argyrou, A., Lambooy, T., & Blomme, R. J. (2017). Inclusive Governance in Social Enterprises in the Netherlands—a Case Study. *Annals of Public and Cooperative Economics, 88*(4), 543–566.

Cook, I. R., & Swyngedouw, E. (2012). Cities, Social Cohesion and the Environment: Towards a Future Research Agenda. *Urban Studies, 49*(9), 1959–1979.

Cooke, P., & Morgan, K. (1998). *Associational Economy: Firms, Regions, And Innovation*. Oxford: Oxford University Press.

CPF. (2018, April). London Declaration on Inclusive Governance for a Renewed Commonwealth. Commonwealth Peoples' Forum 2018, London. Retrieved from http://capgan.info/Associates-Activities/forum-of-commonwealth-health-organition-meetings/CPF-2018-London-Declaration-and-Call-to-Action.pdf

Derven, M. (2014). Diversity and Inclusion by Design: Best Practices from Six Global Companies. *Industrial and Commercial Training, 46*(2), 84–91.

Dobusch, L. (2014). How Exclusive are Inclusive Organisations? *Equality, Diversity and Inclusion, 33*(3), 220–234.

Donovan, M., & Kaplan, M. (2019). *The Inclusion Dividend: Why Investing in Diversity & Inclusion Pays Off.* DG Press.

Edmark, K., & Hanspers, K. (2015). Is Welfare Dependency Inherited? Estimating Causal Welfare Transmission Effects Using Swedish Sibling Data. *European Journal of Social Security, 17*(3), 338–360.

EUKN. (2015). *The Civic Economy: Opportunities and Challenges for European Cities.* The Hague: European Urban Knowledge Network. Retrieved December 4, 2019, from https://www.eukn.eu/fileadmin/Files/Publications/2015_The_Civic_Economy__Opportunities_and_Challenges_for_European_Cities/The_civic_economy.pdf

Falco, E., & Kleinhans, R. (2018). Digital Participatory Platforms for Co-Production in Urban Development: A Systematic Review. *International Journal of E-Planning Research, 7*, 1–27.

Florida, R. (2015, October 5). The New Grand Bargain Between Cities and Anchor Institutions. *CityLab.* Retrieved October 25, 2019, from https://www.citylab.com/equity/2015/10/the-new-grand-bargain-between-cities-and-anchor-institutions/408943/

Florida, R., & McLean, J. W. (2017, July 11). What Inclusive Urban Development Can Look Like. *Harvard Business Review.* Retrieved October 25, 2019, from https://hbr.org/2017/07/what-inclusive-urban-development-can-look-like

Florida, R., & Pedigo, S. (2017). *The Case for Inclusive Prosperity.* NYU—School of Professional Studies. The NYUSPS Schack Institute of Real Estate Urban Lab. Retrieved October 25, 2019, from https://iamstevenpedigo.com/wp-content/uploads/2019/07/NYUSPS-Schack-Urban-Lab-The-Case-for-Inclusive-Prosperity.pdf

Florida, R., Pedigo, S., & Bendix, A. (2018). *Revisiting Inclusive Prosperity.* NYU—School of Professional Studies. The NYUSPS Schack Institute of Real Estate Urban Lab. Retrieved October 25, 2019, from https://iamstevenpedigo.com/wp-content/uploads/2019/07/NYUSPS-Schack-Urban-Lab-The-Case-for-Inclusive-Prosperity.pdf

Franz, B., Skinner, D., Wynn, J., & Kelleher, K. (2019). Urban Hospitals as Anchor Institutions: Frameworks for Medical Sociology. *Socius, 5*, 1–10. https://doi.org/10.1177/2378023118817981

Gibbons, C. (2010). Economic Gardening. *Economic Development Journal, 9*(3), 4–11.

Goldsmith, S., & Kleiman, N. (2017). *A New City O/S: The Power of Open, Collaborative, and Distributed Governance.* Washington, D.C: Brookings Institution Press.

Gonzales, V. (2007). Social Enterprises, Institutional Capacity and Social Inclusion. In A. Noya & E. Clarence (Eds.), *Social Economy: Building Inclusive Economies* (pp. 119–153). Paris: OECD.

Greenwood, D. T., & Holt, R. P. F. (2010). *Local Economic Development in the 21ˢᵗ Century: Quality of Life and Sustainability*. London and New York: Routledge.

Gundling, E., Caldwell, C., & Cvitkovich, K. (2015). *Leading Across New Borders: How to Succeed as the Center Shifts. Aperian Global*. Hoboken, NJ: John Wiley & Sons.

Hasche, N., Höglund, L., & Linton, G. (2019). Quadruple Helix as a Network of Relationships: Creating Value Within a Swedish Regional Innovation System. *Journal of Small Business & Entrepreneurship* (Accepted 6 July 2019). https://doi.org/10.1080/08276331.2019.1643134

Hickey, S., Sen, K., & Bukenya, B. (Eds.). (2015). *The Politics of Inclusive Development: Interrogating the evidence*. Oxford: Oxford University Press.

Hunt, V., Prince, S., Dixon-Fyle, S., & Yee, L. (2018, January). *Delivering through Diversity*. McKinsey & Company. Retrieved December 3, 2019, from https://www.mckinsey.com/~/media/McKinsey/Business%20Functions/Organization/Our%20Insights/Delivering%20through%20diversity/Delivering-through-diversity_full-report.ashx

Kemeny, T., Cooke, A., & Marek Zeitlin, A. (2017, January). The Riches of the Melting Pot: How Diversity in Metropolitan Areas Helps grow the Wages of Low and High-wage Workers. New American Economy, Report. Retrieved December 3, 2019, from http://research.newamericaneconomy.org/wp-content/uploads/2017/02/NAE_Diversity_FINAL.pdf

Lee, D., Loutas, N., Sánchez-Nielsen, E., Mogulkoc, E., & Lacigova, O. (2011). Inform-Consult-Empower: A Three-Tiered Approach to eParticipation. In: E. Tambouris, A. Macintosh, H. de Bruijn (Eds.), *Electronic Participation*. ePart 2011 (Lecture Notes in Computer Science) (Vol. 6847, pp. 121–132). Berlin and Heidelberg: Springer.

Lester, R. K. (2007). Universities, Innovation, and the Competitiveness of Local Economies: An Overview. In R. K. Lester & M. Sotarauta (Eds.), *Innovation, Universities, and the Competitiveness of Regions* (pp. 9–30). Technology Review 214/2007. Helsinki: Tekes.

Malik, F., & Wahaj, Z. (2019). Sharing Economy Digital Platforms and Social Inclusion/Exclusion: A Research Study of Uber and Careem in Pakistan. In P. Nielsen & H. Kimaro (Eds.), *Information and Communication Technologies for Development*. Strengthening Southern-Driven Cooperation as a Catalyst for ICT4D. ICT4D 2019. IFIP Advances in Information and Communication Technology, Vol. 551. Cham: Springer.

OECD. (2015). Policy Shaping and Policy Making: The Governance of Inclusive Growth. Retrieved December 1, 2019, from https://www.oecd.org/governance/ministerial/the-governance-of-inclusive-growth.pdf

Ortlieb, R., & Sieben, B. (2014). The Making of Inclusion as Structuration: Empirical Evidence of a Multinational Company. *Equality, Diversity and Inclusion, 33*(3), 235–248.

Perry, D. C., Wiewel, W., & Menendez, C. (2009, July). The University's Role in Urban Development: From Enclave to Anchor Institution. *Land Lines.* Lincoln Institute of Land Policy. Retrieved December 3, 2019, from https://www.lincolninst.edu/sites/default/files/pubfiles/1647_862_article_1.pdf

Raco, M. (2000). Assessing Community Participation in Local Economic Development—Lessons for the New Urban Policy. *Political Geography, 19*, 573–599.

Reilly, K. (2019, March 12). As the Harvard Admissions Case Nears a Decision, Hear From 2 Asian-American Students on Opposite Sides. *Time.* Retrieved November 21, 2019, from https://time.com/5546463/harvard-admissions-trial-asian-american-students/

Richter, R. (2018). The Janus Face of Participatory Governance: How Inclusive Governance Benefits and Limits the Social Innovativeness of Social Enterprises. *Journal of Entrepreneurial and Organizational Diversity, 7*(1), 61–87.

Rixon, D. (2010). Stakeholder Engagement in Public Sector Agencies: Ascending the Rungs of the Accountability Ladder. *International Journal of Public Administration., 33*(7), 347–356.

Rocha Menocal, A., Power, G., & Kaye, O. (2019). Promoting Inclusive Governance More Effectively: Lessons from the Dialogue for Stability Programme. *Journal of Peacebuilding & Development, 14*(1), 84–89.

Shafique, A., Antink, B., Clay, A., & Cox, E. (2019). *Inclusive Growth in Action: Snapshots of a New Economy.* London: Royal Society for the encouragement of Arts, Manufactures and Commerce (RSA). Retrieved December 7, 2019, from https://www.thersa.org/globalassets/pdfs/reports/rsa-inclusive-growth-in-action.pdf

UNIDO. (2013). Networks for Prosperity: Partnering for Inclusive and Sustainable Industrial Development: Connectedness Index 2014. Published on December 4, 2013. Vienna: Vienna International Centre. United Nations Industrial Development Organization (UNIDO). Retrieved December 1, 2019, from https://issuu.com/unido/docs/network_prosperity_2013_lores

van den Berg, L., Braun, E., & Otgaar, A. H. J. (2004). Corporate Community Involvement in European and US Cities. *Environment and Planning C: Government and Policy, 22*(4), 475–494. https://doi.org/10.1068/c0246

Vickers, I., Westall, A., Spear, R., Brennan, G., & Syrett, S. (2017, June). Cities, the Social Economy and Inclusive Growth: A Practice Review. *Joseph Rowntree Foundation.* Retrieved from https://www.jrf.org.uk/report/cities-social-economy-and-inclusive-growth

World Bank. (2005). Inclusive Governance: Empowering the Poor and Promoting Accountability in Latin America and the Caribbean Region (English).

Washington, DC: World Bank. Retrieved from http://documents.worldbank.
org/curated/en/325671468046167689/
Inclusive-governance-empowering-the-poor-and-promoting-accountability-
in-Latin-America-and-the-Carribbean-Region

CHAPTER 7

Real-Life Cases of Inclusive Urban Development

Abstract This chapter provides an overview of a few real-life examples of inclusive urban development. It begins with a short introduction to various global rankings of inclusive cities, which show that especially liberal and progressive cities in Europe perform well in this regard. This is followed by descriptions of four cities, of which Helsinki and Barcelona are located in Europe, and Portland and Pittsburgh in North America. They all have their specific concerns in terms of the types of exclusion addressed in their policies. Helsinki is an instance of a Nordic welfare society, the Barcelona Model reflects the rise of civic networks and movements, progressive Portland strives for racial equity, and Pittsburgh focuses on restructuration through inclusive innovation.

Keywords Global ranking • Equitable city • Helsinki • Barcelona • Portland • Pittsburgh

Learning from European and American Cities

Although a few short illustrative examples have been mentioned previously, they build only a fragmented view of inclusive city policy. In order to concretize the real-life development in this respect, this chapter delves more systematically into a small number of cases in which forward-looking policies to inclusive urban development, growth, and prosperity have been designed and implemented. Each case illustrates how a city can promote

© The Author(s) 2020
A.-V. Anttiroiko, M. de Jong, *The Inclusive City*,
https://doi.org/10.1007/978-3-030-61365-5_7

inclusive prosperity by involving the interests of excluded or underrepresented groups.

We will first offer a snapshot of the global view of inclusive cities and then take a closer look at a few cities that have approached shared prosperity in a strategic and integrated manner. The selected cases are Helsinki and Barcelona from Europe and Pittsburgh, PA, and Portland, OR, from the USA. The city of Helsinki represents a local instance of the Northern European welfare state context, while Barcelona serves as an example of a Southern European model affected by civic activism and the left-wing municipalism. The two US cases are race and diversity oriented. Portland is a world-renowned green city with progressive urban development agenda, while Pittsburgh utilizes inclusion as a strategic response to its shrinkage challenge and as a means to build a new talent base for its economic restructuring. Discussion about these four cases aims at highlighting different contexts of and responses to local economic development.

The priorities for inclusive urban economy are conditioned by the development level and preconditions of each country (see, e.g., Greene, Pendall, Scott, & Lei, 2016; Harkness, 2019). Accordingly, inclusive city policy is shaped by the societal conditions of each nation, which form a context for local-level challenges and opportunities. Our case cities are located in developed countries, which as a context includes fairly wealthy, technologically advanced, and democratic societies with some features of post-industrial economy and at least some welfare society structures in place. This implies that their preconditions for economic inclusion are relatively good, even if they have their own challenges, too.

GLOBAL OVERVIEW OF INCLUSIVE CITIES

Global Rankings of Inclusive Cities

There is a lack of academic research on this topic, not to mention the availability of global overviews of urban inclusion. Taking this into account, the second-best option for taking a shortcut to a global overview of our topic is rankings. Using a small set of relevant indicators, they put cities into an order, forming thus a snapshot of global urban hierarchy on the basis of the given criteria. One of the few relevant rankings of inclusive prosperity in cities has been published by D&L Partners (2019). Their Inclusive Prosperity Cities Index framework—later renamed *Prosperity and Inclusion in Cities SEAL and Awards Index* or *PICSA Index*—was created to produce metrics for measuring progress and identifying best practices of inclusive prosperity. It is multidimensional ranking based on theoretical developments in this area, such as the work by the OECD (2016). The construct of inclusive prosperity in PICSA Index was conceptualized using three pillars: income; non-monetary well-being of different social groups in society; and the infrastructure and services of cities (D&L Partners, 2019).

According to PICSA Index, the most inclusive cities among the selected 113 cities are located in developed countries, mostly in Europe and a few in Asia (e.g., Taipei) and North America (e.g., Ottawa, Washington, D.C., Seattle, and Boston). The most highly ranked cities are presented in Table 7.1.

Another ranking that illustrates inclusive urban development is *Open for Business* report, which ranks cities according to the indicators of global LGBT+ inclusion. It has a rather normative tone, but provides in any case

Table 7.1 Top 20 inclusive cities

No	City	Points
1	Zurich	78.2
2	Vienna	72.0
3	Copenhagen	70.5
4	Luxembourg	70.3
5	Helsinki	70.1
6	Taipei	69.9
7	Oslo	69.8
8	Ottawa	69.8
9	Kiel	69.5
10	Geneva	68.3
11	Washington, D.C.	68.2
12	Munich	68.2
13	Prague	66.8
14	Seattle	66.6
15	Stockholm	66.0
16	Boston	65.8
17	Amsterdam	65.2
18	Berlin	65.0
19	Eindhoven	64.2
20	Bilbao	64.0

Source: D&L Partners (2019)

empirical evidence to support its view of the state of affairs. The report demonstrates that successful businesses thrive in diverse and inclusive societies, for, as the statistics show, inclusion has a positive correlation with GDP per capita and innovativeness. The city ranking presented in the report combines 23 metrics that cover social, legal, and economic factors, including attitudes toward sexual orientation and gender identity, city LGBT+ inclusion score, support from city officials, and LGBT+ legal situation. The report gives 121 cities A, B, C, and D ratings, each having three sub-divisions, plus an extra rating E, which indicates a closed city (Miller & Parker, 2018). These ratings are presented in Table 7.2.

As a third relevant ranking we may bring forth the *2018 Millennial Cities Ranking* by Nestpick. It measures business ecosystem, amenities and basic services, openness, and recreation, in which 100 capitals and economic and ex-pat hubs are analyzed in order to illustrate how attractive they are to a younger generation. Globally most highest ranked cities are Berlin, Montreal, London, Amsterdam, Toronto, Vancouver, Barcelona, New York City, Cologne, and Manchester. Regarding inclusion-related subcategories, in *gender equality* scores are high in cities in Nordic countries, Ireland, and New Zealand. *Immigration tolerance* reaches its highest level in cities in New Zealand, Canada, and Norway. Most *LGBT friendly cities* include Madrid, Amsterdam, Toronto, Berlin, Montreal, Bristol, London, Cologne, Vancouver, and Munich (Nestpick, 2018).

There are also some country-level rankings and indexes that as broader contexts provide perspective to the development of cities. For example, the *Social Progress Index (SPI)*, published by the non-profit Social Progress Imperative (https://www.socialprogress.org/), measures how countries meet the social and environmental needs of their citizens, using 54 indicators that reflect basic human needs, well-being, and opportunity to progress. On the basis of national development, the globally most advanced cities are located in Nordic countries, Switzerland, and white Commonwealth countries.

Social cohesion is one of the dimensions in *IESE Cities in Motion Index 2019*, which measures societal features that are relevant for inclusiveness. In the urban context, it refers to the aspects of coexistence among groups of people with different incomes, cultures, ages, and professions. Measuring this dimension included 16 indicators, such as Gini index, female workers, price of property, Global Peace Index, happiness index, Global Slavery Index, terrorism, crime rate, and suicides. In this ranking, 174 cities from

Table 7.2   Open for Business city ratings

Open for Business city ratings of selected cities in developed and developing countries

City is fully open for business	AAA	Amsterdam, Berlin, Chicago, Dublin, London, New York City, San Francisco, Stockholm, Toronto, Washington, D.C.
	AA	Boston, Helsinki, Los Angeles, Madrid, Melbourne, Minneapolis, Montreal, Paris, Sydney, Vancouver
	A	Atlanta, Auckland (NZ), Barcelona, Birmingham, UK, Calgary, Dallas, Edinburgh, Frankfurt, Glasgow, Hamburg, Houston, Munich, Ottawa, Stuttgart, Wellington
City is partially open for business	BBB	Adelaide, Belfast, Brisbane, Lisbon, Lyon, Perth, Singapore, Tel Aviv, Tokyo
	BB	Buenos Aires, Hong Kong, Osaka, Santiago, Sao Paulo, Yokohama
	B	Bangalore, Cape Town, Guadalajara, Medellin, Mexico City, Milan, Nagoya, Rio de Janeiro, Rome, Seoul, Warsaw
	CCC	Athens, Bogota, Bucharest, Budapest, Busan, Durban, Ho Chi Minh City, Wroclaw, Zagreb
	CC	Bangkok, Belgrade, Brasilia, Johannesburg, Manila, Mumbai, New Delhi
	C	Abu Dhabi, Beijing, Chennai, Dubai, Hyderabad, Kuala Lumpur, Shanghai, Tirana
City is not open for business	DDD	Guangzhou, Hanoi, Istanbul, Kiev, Kingston, Skopje
	DD	Amman, Chongqing, Colombo, Jakarta, Moscow, Sarajevo
	D	Almaty, Casablanca, Dakar, Dhaka, Nairobi, Rabat
	E	Addis Ababa, Algiers, Baku, Cairo, Dar Es Salaam, Douala, Jeddah, Karachi, Lagos, Lahore, Riyadh, Tehran

Keys: AAA, Global Beacon; AA, Prime; A, High; BBB, Upper Medium; BB, Medium; B, Lower Medium; CCC, Rather Low; CC, Low; C, Very Low; DDD, Medium Risk; DD, Substantial Risk; D, High Risk; E, Closed.

Source: Adopted from Miller and Parker (2018, p. 37)

80 countries were analyzed. Top 10 cities in terms of social cohesion in 2019 ranking included Zurich, Bern, Taipei, Basel, Wellington, Quebec, Abu Dhabi, Eindhoven, and Helsinki (IESE Business School, 2019).

Urban Geography of Social and Economic Inclusion

Previous rankings show some degree of saturation in terms of where we can find the most inclusive cities. In this regard, the most notable fact is the leading role of progressive *European cities*. We can say that Europe is the continent of most inclusive cities in the world, as shown by PICSA Index with Zurich, Vienna, Copenhagen, Luxemburg, and Helsinki as Top 5, and Open for Business ratings, in which Amsterdam, Dublin, Berlin, London, and Stockholm have the highest AAA rating, followed by Madrid, Helsinki, and Paris each with AA rating. In another ranking produced by Savills Investment Management of the most innovative, inspiring, and inclusive cities among 130 European capitals and metropolitan areas with at least quarter of a million inhabitants, the highest scores were obtained by London, Paris, Cambridge, Amsterdam, Berlin, Munich, Dublin, Stockholm, Edinburgh, Zurich, Madrid, Vienna, Oslo, Oxford, Basel, Lausanne, and Barcelona (Fitzmaurice, 2017).

Another group of cities worth special mention comes from *the USA and white Commonwealth countries*, of which the latter—including the UK from Europe, Canada from North America, and New Zealand and Australia from Australasia—are fairly well-positioned in terms of social and economic inclusion, while the US cities have slightly more polarized structures and more pronounced diversity policies due to country's historical heritage and high awareness of racial and identity political sensitivities. Cities within these countries have special strengths in freedom, inclusion, and diversity, as shown in previously mentioned Open for Business ratings (Miller & Parker, 2018). There is a ranking of US cities in terms of changes in economic and racial inclusion, which shows that especially California is a home of many cities that show good results in economic inclusion (Poethig, Greene, Stacy, Srini, & Meixell, 2018; see also Florida, 2012; Misra, 2018).

There are several other groups of cities in *developed countries*, which are fairly prosperous, well-functioning, and technologically advanced, including cities from Eastern European countries like Estonia, Hungary, and the Czech Republic, East Asian countries like Japan and South Korea, and wealthy oil-producing countries, such as the UAE (incl. Dubai), Qatar, and Bahrain. Many cities of these three groups are in the middle rank in the previously mentioned inclusive city ranking, of which illustrative examples are Tallinn (22), Budapest (55), Osaka (44), Seoul (49), Nagoya (71), Dubai (63), and Kuwait City (77). A notable exception to this rule is formed by Arab and North African and also several other countries in which Islam is the politically defined state religion, which have several restrictions of personal freedom and serious violations of the rights of women and LGBT+ people.

Western cities are in many occasions contrasted with their most powerful rivals on a global economic scene, those of emerging global cities in Asia. *China* with its surging global cities makes a case in point. As put in A.T. Kearney's (2019) global cities report, Chinese cities need to explore how they can create more open-minded and inclusive policies that protect the rights of all citizens, regardless of their religion, sexual orientation, or income (A.T. Kearney, 2019). Situation is even more critical with *India*'s most global cities—such as capital city of Delhi, financial center Mumbai, and high-tech hot spot Bangalore (officially Bengaluru)—as they are among the world's least inclusive cities according to previously mentioned PISCA Index (Chandar, 2019).

HELSINKI: A WELFARIST APPROACH TO SOCIAL AND ECONOMIC INCLUSION

Helsinki is the capital of Finland, which is one of the five Nordic countries in the northern part of Europe. The city has some 650,000 inhabitants. Together with surrounding cities, it forms the country's most important metropolitan area with the biggest concentration of business services, higher education, and creative industries.

Inclusion has an important role in Helsinki's City Strategy 2017–2021. As formulated in the strategy, Helsinki presents itself as a functional city with strong emphasis on equality, non-discrimination, social cohesion, and open and inclusive ways of operating. City strategy starts from the conviction that Helsinki as a city is for everyone and that it is built together.

Helsinki has two-sided *economic development policy* in the sense that its objective is to be one of Europe's most captivating locations for innovative start-ups and the most attractive knowledge hub for companies and individuals wanting to make the world a better place to live in, while relying on new models of sharing economy created by residents and companies that make the city economically diverse and inclusive.

Another aspect of economic development is to promote the match between the skills and talent of residents and *employment opportunities*. The City Strategy emphasizes that "[t]he city's measures and services to promote employment are especially directed towards those groups where participation in the labour market is lowest." In addition, the city underlines investment in education, employment, and inclusion for second-generation immigrants, in particular. Even if Helsinki is not particularly diverse city by European standards, it has given immigrants a high priority in its strategic development: "Qualifications that immigrants have acquired in their country of origin are identified and acknowledged flexibly, and the skills of immigrants are, whenever possible, put to the labour market's disposal. Entrepreneurship is encouraged as one way of finding employment" (City of Helsinki, n.d.).

Lastly, according to City Strategy, Helsinki wants to strengthen its position as an *international forerunner in inclusion and transparency*. It wants all the residents to feel that they are full-fledged citizens empowered to do significant things for their city. The Strategy stresses that "[t]he city strives to maintain the trust of residents and companies, to strengthen their real influence and to improve equality, service standards and mutual understanding between population groups through modern models of inclusion." Moreover, just like in other Nordic countries, gender equality is a principle permeating all activities of the city (City of Helsinki, n.d.).

How do these principles turn into reality? A kind of mediating institutional tool between strategy and action is a Helsinki Participation and Interaction Model, accepted by the City's Management Board on November 13, 2017. The model is built on three principles: the utilization of the know-how and expertise of individuals and communities; enabling of spontaneous activities; and the provision of equal opportunities for participation (specified in the Administrative Ordinance of the City, formally accepted by the City Council on November 16, 2016). (Helsingin kaupunki, 2019). The key elements of the Participation and Interaction Model are illustrated in Fig. 7.1.

While many aspects of the model operate within conventional participatory democracy, it has elements that relate to special value creation processes and activities associated with *economic inclusion*. An example is a

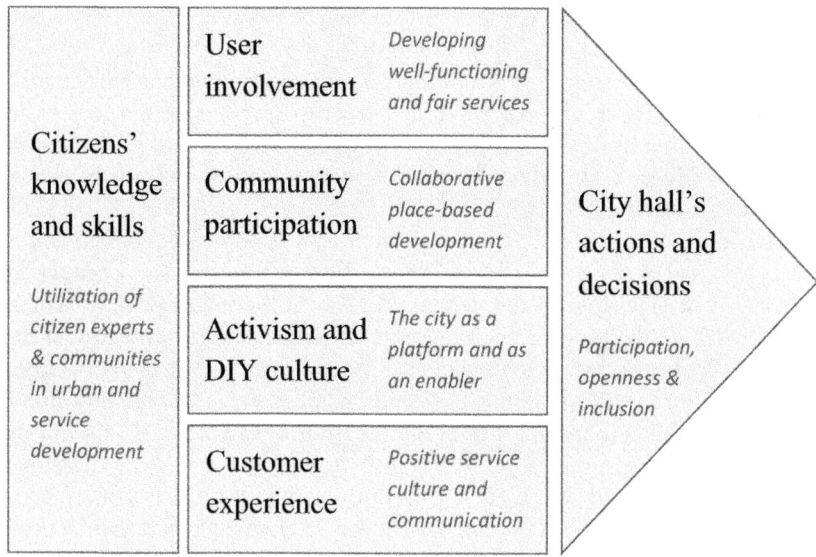

Fig. 7.1 Key aspects of Helsinki's Participation and Interaction Model

new model for volunteer activities, which focuses on volunteering opportunities, collaboration with local associations, and nine city government's coordinators and some 60 part-time instructors that support volunteering in different sectors. The other area in which city government aims at supporting value creation is the application of the principle that all the public premises owned by the city government are available for citizens to be reserved through digital reservation service site. The city has also started to utilize participatory budgeting in the development of different districts of the city, facilitated by "city couches" designated to seven city districts. Beside this, there are three business couches whose task is to facilitate the initiatives of businesses and promote employment and business opportunities in different city districts.

Another pillar of economic inclusion is directed toward higher value-adding activities. These activities are addressed in the economic development plan of the city for 2018–2021. It contains three strategic areas: (i) increasing international attractiveness, (ii) attracting and nurturing talent, and (iii) serving as a platform for growth. Regarding talent, the role of immigrants has been given a high priority. In the development of the city as a platform, the aim is to develop Helsinki as the world's most advanced public sector ecosystem by combining the means of digitalization, design, and inclusion (Helsingin kaupunki, 2018). Instrumental to this goal is the City of Helsinki innovation company, Forum Virium Helsinki. Its mission is to make Helsinki the most functional smart city in the world (https://forumvirium.fi/en/).

Helsinki's efforts toward economic inclusion are not necessarily as radical as let's say in some US cities. This can be explained by two contextual factors. First, Helsinki is the capital of a Finnish welfare society, which means that public policies are inherently directed toward ensuring sufficient level of economic inclusion. The other factor is that in the Nordic countries there is a long cherished solidaristic tradition of focusing more on citizens' rights than their duties or contributions, which still conditions the policies of Helsinki and other Finnish cities. This is why the measures geared toward value creation and economic inclusion are not as pronounced as the activities that aim at promoting citizen participation, social welfare, and human rights.

BARCELONA: CIVIC MOVEMENTS AND NETWORKS AS INCLUSIVE CITY CATALYSTS

Barcelona is a dynamic city with some 1.7 million inhabitants within city limits and some 5.6 million in the larger metropolitan area. It rose in the wake of the restoration of Spanish democracy, which decentralized the political structure of the country. Barcelona's success on the European scene since the 1990s reflects a continuity of long-lasted power of left-wing parties and the rise of activism and civic movements. Another critical background factor is the broad-based commitment to the modernization of the city, spurring the revitalization of its cultural and economic dynamism. Such an approach became known as the Barcelona model, one of its symbolic milestones being the 1992 Olympic Games. The city started to pursue inclusion-oriented welfare city model without losing sight of the critical role of economic vitality and growth (Montagut, Vilà, & Riutort, 2016). Let us discuss next how the city government created positive synergies between citizen-centeredness, entrepreneurship, and technological development and utilized it in its strategic inclusion agenda.

Barcelona provided support to entrepreneurship since the establish-ment of its economic development agency Barcelona Activa (BA) in 1986. However, its current Inclusive Entrepreneurship Model (IEM) was designed in 2004 with a mission to make entrepreneurship a realistic option for everyone, thus creating jobs and raising people's economic and social autonomy. Barriers to entrepreneurship are high among such groups as women, youth, and those over 45 years old. To address such challenges, BA set up the IEM as an integrated support to everyone willing to become an entrepreneur with a special focus on the most vulnerable population that may not benefit from conventional business services. The IEM com-bines the economic and social views using physical and online channels to provide services and to offer coaching while utilizing the city's ecosystem. The results of the model between 2004 and 2016 include serving more than 100,000 people, 3800 of them within tailor-made programs, gener-ating some 26,000 business plans and assisting the establishment of some 18,000 enterprises, which created over 30,000 jobs (URBACT, n.d.).

A more recent move toward inclusive and socially oriented entrepre-neurship was the establishment of InnoBA in 2018, an integral part of the municipal strategy to provide resources for the Social and Solidarity Economy (SSE). The city views SSE as a driving force in the transforma-tion toward a fair city. SS E is broadly understood as the group of organi-zations with explicit social objectives, including cooperatives, mutual benefit societies, foundations, and social enterprises as well as informal initiatives and citizens' movements that are geared to democratize the economy (Papadaki & Kalogeraki, 2018). SSE is estimated to represent about 7% of Barcelona's GDP and expected to grow in the coming years. One of the major facilitating structures of InnoBA is La innoBadora, the city's fifth business incubator and the first one to specialize in SSE proj-ects. Regarding SSE, the city has paid a lot of attention to entrepreneur-ship programs for women-led projects and SSE organizations. There are programs for other special groups as well, such as those designed for youth.

The city has strong emphasis on direct citizen involvement in public governance. A social innovation that reflects such a thinking is Citizen's Agreement for an Inclusive Barcelona (CA). It was established in April 2005. The ultimate goal of the program is to redistribute responsibilities in the social welfare sector in Barcelona through a broad agreement among representatives of the local associations, enterprises, and institutions. It enables shared goal setting, opportunity enhancement, and coordination, including more than 600 collaborators to date. The signing of the agreement means that collaborators join networks that facilitate access to and exchange of information, resources, and knowledge and involvement in socially motivated collaborative projects. Such thematic networks are characteristic to the governance style associated with the Barcelona model (Montagut et al., 2016).

In order to coordinate the sectoral and geographic policies in the purpose of ensuring the delivery of services for the inclusion of citizens, the city drafted the Barcelona Social Inclusion Plan for 2012–2015. It was a main tool for the City Council in its pursue toward an inclusive and cohesive city in which everyone is provided conditions for a good life and which combats the exclusion tendencies that prevail in the city. The plan contained four strategic lines: (a) an inclusive local authority; (b) an inclusive and cohesive city; (c) people and neighborhoods; and (d) civil society and citizenship. In the realization of the strategic actions the role of networks is essential, most notably in involving civil society in urban development. The networks were organized according to key themes, including Social Economy Network, Social Inclusion Housing Network, Culture for Social Inclusion Network, and Reception and Support Network for Immigrants (on the Plan for Social Inclusion, Barcelona 2012–2015, see http://www. bcn.cat/plainclusiosocial/en/index.shtml) (Montagut et al., 2016).

It is noteworthy that as citizen-oriented as Barcelona is, it does not focus only on citizen rights or inclusion as a human right, but also on the economic side of inclusion, most notably supporting access to employment and entrepreneurial activity (Broadhead, 2017). At the heart of Barcelona's immigration policy are activities for training immigrants and helping them join the workforce (Garcés-Mascareñas, 2014; Gebhardt, 2016). As these kinds of policies concern primarily only a particular group of inhabitants and have become mainstreamed during the last few decades, we do not touch upon them in this chapter. There is a more fundamental aspect to be elaborated. Namely, the transformation of the economic structure of the city of Barcelona from an industrial city into a knowledge-intensive hub or a smart city has successfully encouraged entrepreneurship and business growth with strong social dimension in it (URBACT, n.d.). In short, the Barcelona model has evolved from a conventional "worlding" vision with techno-economic focus toward its radical repurposing under the auspices of a municipal government led by the left-wing grassroots movement called Barcelona en Comú and then new mayor Ada

Colau since the mid-2010s. The new government started to work for a new strategic plan for Barcelona through a process that was to become the "most participative strategic plan in the history of the city." An innovative vehicle for deciding a new plan was Decidim Barcelona, a web-based platform developed at Barcelona's Laboratory for Democratic Innovation, which was blended with real-world engagement to avoid exclusion (Shafique, Antink, Clay, & Cox, 2019). It is noteworthy that the City Council started to co-govern with civil society and was committed to utilize digital platform technologies to revitalize democracy (Charnock, March, & Ribera-Fumaz, 2019). Along with this process, the smart city concept transformed into popular and democratic view of innovation and entrepreneurship, as seen in the work of urban innovation labs in the city (Ferrer, 2017). Another indication of a paradigm shift was the increased focus on SSE, re-municipalization of resources, and democratization of technological infrastructure and data, including the promotion of co-operative business models and the use of public procurement to steward local economy in new ways (Shafique et al., 2019). The new democratic structures are galvanizing efforts to rebalance economic power in the city. The reforms in Barcelona are part of a wider global movement that aims at creating a shift toward a progressive municipalism with the commitment to promote the rise of new bottom-up centers of power and value creation.

PORTLAND: STRATEGIC RACE-SENSITIVE POLICY FOR SHARED PROSPERITY

Portland is the largest city in the state of Oregon in the USA. Its estimated population is around 650,000, while the number of inhabitants in the larger metropolitan statistical area is around 2.4 million. Portland is known for the urban growth boundary, land-use planning, and advanced public transportation. Its brand revolves around sustainable development. Portland has made notable progress with social and economic inclusion as well.

There are demographic and economic factors that have given impetus of radical initiative in promoting economic inclusion. Namely, Portland is one of the US metros that will experience the most dramatic demographic shift in the near future, implying that large part of the workforce will be people of color. While people of color make today less than 30% of the city's population, almost 50% of current students—and thus the future workforce—in Portland's public schools are children of color. It is imperative to see social and economic inclusion as a precondition for long-term economic development. Another similar premise is that the lack of diversity is not good for innovativeness. In general, a high level of innovation correlates with companies with diverse teams. Moreover, another general premise is that economic inequities tend to diminish economic growth in the long run. This speaks for progressive policies that aim at increasing social and economic inclusion of blacks, Hispanics, and other minority groups. Equitable city will attract an increasingly diverse workforce who view Portland as a place where everyone can succeed. On the basis of these kinds of premises, the goal of Portland's Strategic Plan 2015–2020 is to achieve widely shared prosperity among all residents of the city (Portland Development Commission, n.d.). In order to attain the goal of widely shared prosperity among all residents, the city of Portland is committed to give an equal emphasis on building healthy communities, maintaining economic competitiveness, and creating equitable opportunities, as depicted in Fig. 7.2.

Portland's economic development agency has dedicated to the active promotion of inclusion. The unit in question is *Prosper Portland* (https://

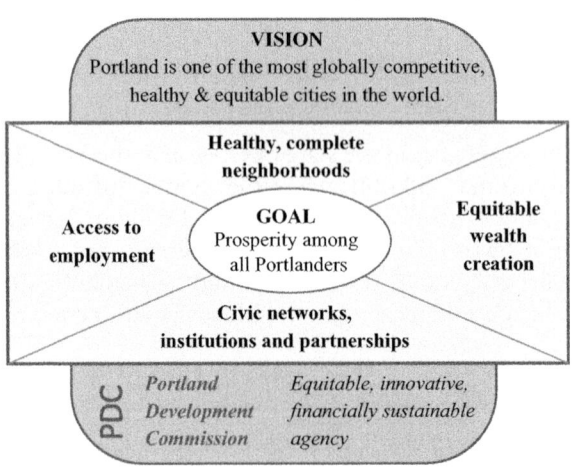

Fig. 7.2 The vision and goal of Portland's economic development. (Source: Adopted from Portland Development Commission, n.d., p. 10)

prosperportland.us/). While it has a conventional mission due to its role in the line organization of city government, its strong emphasis on building an equitable economy makes it unique by global comparison. While it is committed to growing quality jobs, advancing opportunities for prosperity, creating vibrant neighborhoods and communities, just like any local development agency, it does this in order to create an equitable city, with prosperity shared by Portlanders of all colors, incomes, and neighborhoods. The mission, vision, and values of Prosper Portland are centered in racial equity and serve as the foundation for the Equity Framework, which guides the implementation of the strategic plan and actions. This sentiment is expressed in the Equity Statement of Prosper Portland.

Equity Statement

We acknowledge our past as we move forward to create economic opportunity and prosperity for all communities. We make racial equity the foundation of our community and economic development work. We hold ourselves accountable to Portland's communities of color and others our work has negatively impacted. While racial equity is the primary lens to focus our efforts, we understand the connection between racism and other forms of bias that lead to oppression.

Within our workplace and working with our partners, we embrace values of authentic inclusion, transparency, and collaboration.

We work toward nothing less than an anti-racist Portland that welcomes and serves all communities and perspectives. We encourage our partners to do the same.

Source: Prosper Portland (2019, p. 7)

In the given context, "[e]quity is when everyone has access to the opportunity necessary to satisfy their essential needs, advance their well-being and achieve their full potential" (Prosper Portland, 2019). Paying attention to equity is based on the following premises: (1) because opportunities currently do not exist for everyone, equity is a restorative measure of redistributing benefits and burdens; (2) because as individuals we operate within systems that create inequities, equity requires both individual and systems-level change; and (3) because "business as usual" will not change by itself, equity requires transforming the culture that produces different outcomes of the organization. The focus on equity implies that treating everyone in the same way is not enough; rather it is to ensure that everyone has what they need to be successful (Prosper Portland, 2019).

The work of the city of Portland in equity-oriented economic development and shared prosperity can be traced back to the latter half of the 2000s. This development is documented in a range of documents and actions, such as the Business & Workforce Equity Policy (adopted 2007); the Economic Development Strategy (2009); the Neighborhood Economic Development Strategy (2011); the Equity Policy (2013); and the 2015–2020 Strategic Plan. The Equity Policy, which has been updated in 2017 and 2019, is of vital importance in guiding such actions. It calls for all projects, initiatives, and investments to generate equitable outcomes and establishes a multicultural, anti-racist institutional framework for the Prosper Portland (Prosper Portland, 2019).

Prosper Portland is an agency that strives to create a culture of putting people first, collaboration, inclusion, learning, excellence, and innovation. In order to ensure that it builds an equitable economy that makes concrete improvement in the lives of people of color and those historically underserved, Prosper Portland focuses on five main efforts of its 2020 Strategic Plan, each point reflecting the tone of equity framework:

1. Growing quality jobs
2. Advancing opportunities for prosperity
3. Collaborating with partners for an equitable city
4. Creating vibrant neighborhoods and communities
5. Operating as an equitable and effective steward of public resources

Prosper Portland delivers its work primarily through programs and investments with a focus on inclusive growth and addressing persistent gaps. It leads with race as the primary factor in determining outcomes for the community, and prioritizes its resources accordingly (Prosper Portland, 2019).

PITTSBURGH: PLANNING FOR INCLUSIVE INNOVATION

Pittsburgh is a city with some 300,000 inhabitants in the city proper in the state of Pennsylvania in the USA. Together with the surrounding areas its metropolitan area population is around 2.3 million. It was for long known as "the Steel City" due to its industrial heritage, which was dramatically affected by the decline of heavy industries and the moving out of local companies in the 1970s and the following decade. This led to a major demographic shift, for the population dropped from a peak of 675,000 in 1950 to 370,000 in 1990. The city has put serious efforts to restructure its economy and, consequently, it is on its way to transform itself into a service and technology hub.

In terms of economic inclusion, Pittsburgh's preconditions for development have been anything but promising. Its restructuring process has, however, shown signs of hope. Unlike most American cities, in which digital tasks and skills have been unevenly spread across the economy, Pittsburgh together with a few other metropolitan areas has been able to include women, people of color, and workers without a college degree in technology occupations. This is important message as high-tech as an industrial sector has not usually been conducive to inclusive prosperity as such.

Whiton and Muro's (2018) analysis of digitally inclusive technology cities reveals that Pittsburgh's strong performance on tech inclusivity—its black and Hispanic underrepresentation in computer and math occupations hovering at -3.7% and -0.2%, respectively—is particularly impressive given its history as a blue-collar steel town. This is partly due to the determination of the city in working proactively toward digital inclusion, as pointed out by its *Roadmap for Inclusive Innovation* initiative launched in 2015. In addition, under the auspices of *Inclusive Innovation PGH*, which is a joint collaboration between the City of Pittsburgh, the Department of Innovation & Performance, and the Urban Redevelopment Authority, the City hosts an annual Inclusive Innovation Week offering free events on the myriad private and non-profit efforts to make inclusion and diversity a priority in tech entrepreneurship and hiring (Whiton & Muro, 2018).

Taken into account the specific challenges of Pittsburgh, it placed *immigrants* at the heart of its growth aspirations and chose inclusion as one of its strategic aims. This can be largely explained by the dramatic population decline during the decades of deindustrialization. The new policy aims at growing the population by 20,000 over the next 10 years. This policy is integrated with the city's economic growth plan and has given high priority to working with existing community groups rather than setting up new attraction-oriented initiatives (Broadhead, 2017).

An epitome of this policy was the previously mentioned *Roadmap for Inclusive Innovation*, a strategic plan launched on the basis of the vision of Mayor William Peduto for making Pittsburgh "a city of equity, access and opportunity through cross-sector partnerships and collaboration." The objective of the Roadmap was to provide a vision for Pittsburgh's future, which is in essence about ensuring that it is possible for everyone to participate in developing and delivering new solutions as well as to benefit from them. It relies heavily on the idea of collaboration, based on the conviction that bringing diverse people together includes a huge potential for problem-solving and innovation.

Even if the Roadmap was authored by the Department of Innovation & Performance and the Urban Redevelopment Authority's Center for Innovation and Entrepreneurship, its creation was a collaborative effort, including various city departments and local partners (City of Pittsburgh, n.d.). The Roadmap for Inclusive Innovation (2015–2018) was broken down into the following focal areas: (i) addressing the digital divide; (ii) empowering city-to-citizen engagement; (iii) providing open data to Pittsburgh; (iv) improving internal operations and capacity of the City; (v) advancing the clean tech sector; and (vi) promoting the local business environment. Each section dealt with a unique set of goals and actions to meet those goals. In practice, the work was organized as projects designed to improve the City's online services, enhance digital literacy, and create new opportunities for local entrepreneurs (City of Pittsburgh, n.d.). All the actions within these six focus areas have been clearly defined and their implementation has been evaluated (see at https://weinnovatepgh.net/roadmap/).

The Roadmap was a landmark in the economic inclusion policy of Pittsburgh. It was conducive to branding Pittsburgh as an Inclusive Innovation City, which helps in promoting the city as an inclusive center for creative industries. Regarding the future of inclusion policy, as some of the actions were not finished by the summer 2018 when the Roadmap was closed, they were continued through the purview of OnePGH Resilient Pittsburgh, a strategy for the city to thrive in the twenty-first century. Concerning other aspects of the Roadmap, they have been refined and developed further through the Inclusive Innovation Summit and Meetups, organized by Inclusive Innovation PGH.

Concluding Remarks

A key common denominator of the four cases discussed above is that in their case inclusion is part of their city strategy and strategic urban economic development. At the same time, each of them has their unique context-specific features.

In Helsinki inclusion is integrated in the city strategy and daily operations within a democratic system as a cross-cutting principle. Helsinki aims at being the most "functional city" in the world, which implies that its inclusion is integrated into a broader policy framework. In Barcelona the role of civil society and popular left-wing politics has been decisive, fused with modernization and the democratization of technology, which provide new tools to inclusion. The Barcelona Model highlights the role of civil society and citizen involvement, collaborative networks, and Social and Solidarity Economy. Portland in Oregon is an example of a progressive American city, which strives for becoming an "equitable city." Prosper Portland is the key organization that is dedicated to foster economic inclusion. The city of Pittsburgh in Pennsylvania utilizes inclusion strategically to compensate its population decline and to restructure its economy. The city has integrated inclusionary actions into its innovation-driven economic development policy, epitomized in the label "Inclusive Innovation City." The features of the strategic approaches to the idea of inclusive city of the abovementioned cities are depicted in Table 7.3.

In Western cities, economic inclusion has become a multidimensional issue that thrives at the intersection of three pillars: citizen-centric governance, technology enhancement, and economic value creation. Regarding the varieties of approaches to urban economic inclusion, we may hypothesize that in homogeneous societies inclusion can be integrated into urban governance and service systems, while in the context where there is distrust in democratic institutions, attention is directed either to civil society or business. In the case of Barcelona, for example, the alignment with civil society is crucial. In diverse and polarized contexts, as in many US cities, approach to inclusion is often built along racial lines with strong connection with identity politics, which tends to lead to specific inclusionary programs.

Table 7.3 Special features of four case cities' approaches to economic inclusion

City/ Criteria	Helsinki	Barcelona	Portland	Pittsburgh
Context	A capital city of a homogeneous Nordic welfare society; egalitarianism; in the post-war decades strong influence of social democracy	A progressive city in Mediterranean Europe; democratization of Spain in the 1970s; critical role of civic and left-leaning grassroots movements	Progressive green city on the Pacific coast (USA); a growing city, known for its livability and environmental friendliness, yet inequality is on the rise	A US city at the western frontier of the Northeast; Steel City heritage; challenges of deindustrialization, population decline, and ethnic diversity
Strategic lines	City Strategy: "Functional city"; Helsinki Participation and Interaction Model; economic development plan	Strategic city plan; Citizen's Agreement for an Inclusive Barcelona (CA); Social Inclusion Plan (2012); Inclusive Entrepreneurship Model (IEM); special attention to Social and Solidarity Economy (SSE)	Portland's strategic plan 2015–2020: "Equitable city"; Equity Statement of Prosper Portland; focus on people of color in workforce and innovation; anti-racism	Roadmap for Inclusive Innovation (2015); city is building itself as an "Inclusive Innovation City"; OnePGH Resilient Pittsburgh
Organization	City government; Forum Virium Helsinki	Barcelona model and network governance; Decidim Barcelona platform; Barcelona Activa; InnoBA; La InnoBadora and other urban innovation labs	Portland Development Commission; Prosper Portland; strategic reliance on networks, institutions, and partnerships	Inclusive Innovation PGH; the Department of Innovation and Performance; Urban Redevelopment Authority; partnerships and collaboration

(*continued*)

Table 7.3   (continued)

City/ Criteria	Helsinki	Barcelona	Portland	Pittsburgh
Examples of actions	Inclusion as a cross-cutting theme; support to volunteering; business coaches	Actions initiated by thematic networks; citizens' initiatives through platforms; training immigrants; entrepreneurship programs for women-led projects	Partnerships for an equitable city; neighborhood development; programs with focus on inclusive growth	Project aiming at improving digital literacy; open data; Inclusive Innovation Summit and Meetups

References

Broadhead, J. (2017). *Inclusive Cities: Inclusive Practices for Newcomers at City Level and Examples of Innovation from Overseas.* The Centre on Migration, Policy and Society (COMPAS), University of Oxford. Retrieved December 15, 2019, from https://www.compas.ox.ac.uk/wp-content/uploads/Inclusive-Cities-Background-Paper-Oct-2017-FINAL.pdf

Chandar, S. (2019, November 22). Bengaluru, Delhi, and Mumbai are Some of the Least Inclusive Global Cities. *Quartz India.* Retrieved December 15, from https://qz.com/india/1754048/bengaluru-delhi-and-mumbai-among-least-inclusive-global-cities/

Charnock, G., March, H., & Ribera-Fumaz, R. (2019). From Smart to Rebel City? Worlding, Provincialising and the Barcelona Model. *Urban Studies.* First Published October 9, 2019. https://doi.org/10.1177/0042098019872119

City of Helsinki. (n.d.). The Most Functional City in the World: Helsinki City Strategy 2017–2021. Retrieved December 17, 2019, from https://www.hel.fi/helsinki/en/administration/strategy/strategy/city-strategy/

City of Pittsburgh. (n.d.). Pittsburgh Roadmap for Inclusive Innovation. Retrieved December 17, 2019, from https://pittsburghpa.gov/innovation-performance/innovationroadmap/documents/Pittsburgh-Roadmap-for-Inclusive-Innovation.pdf

D&L Partners. (2019, February). Creating an Inclusive Prosperity Cities Index: Background and Methodology. Retrieved December 14, 2019, from https://www.picsaindex.com/wp-content/uploads/2019/11/Creating-an-Inclusive-Prosperity-Cities-Index-final-PICSA-report_Nov2019.pdf

Ferrer, J.-R. (2017). Barcelona's Smart City Vision: An Opportunity for Transformation. *Field Actions Science Reports, Special Issue, 16,* 70–75.

Fitzmaurice, R. (2017, June 28). The 17 Most Inclusive Cities in Europe. *Business Insider.* Retrieved December 19, 2019, from https://www.businessinsider.com/the-most-dynamic-cities-in-europe-2017-6?r=UK

Florida, R. (2012, July 16). The Geography of Tolerance. *CityLab.* Retrieved December 19, 2019, from https://www.citylab.com/equity/2012/07/geography-tolerance/2241/

Garcés-Mascareñas, B. (2014, October 12). Local Integration Policies in Barcelona. KING Project—Social Science Unit. In-depth Study n. Retrieved December 21, 2019, from https://ec.europa.eu/migrant-integration/?action=media.download&uuid=2A711DF4-B99D-6188-A2138147797F253A

Gebhardt, D. (2016). Re-thinking Urban Citizenship for Immigrants from a Policy Perspective: The Case of Barcelona. *Citizenship Studies, 20*(6–7), 846–866. https://doi.org/10.1080/13621025.2016.1191431

Greene, S., Pendall, R., Scott, M. M., & Lei, S. (2016). *Open Cities: From Economic Exclusion to Urban Inclusion.* Washington, DC: Urban Institute. Retrieved December 17, 2019, from https://www.urban.org/research/publication/open-cities-economic-exclusion-urban-inclusion

Harkness, A. (2019, May 30). Inclusive Urban Economic Development: A Framework For Action. The 2018 Chicago Forum on Global Cities, June 7, 2018. *Chicago Council on Global Affairs.* Retrieved December 17, 2019, from https://www.thechicagocouncil.org/sites/default/files/report_inclusive-urban-economic-development-framework-for-action_20190530.pdf

Helsingin kaupunki. (2018). Helsingin elinkeinopolitiikan painopisteet 2018–2021 [Focuses of the economic development policy of Helsinki 2018–2021]. Helsingin kaupunginkanslia, Elinkeino-osasto. Retrieved December 21, 2019, from https://www.hel.fi/static/kanslia/elo/Elinkeinopolitiikan-painopisteet-2018-2021.pdf

Helsingin kaupunki. (2019, December 5). Osallisuus- ja vuorovaikutusmalli [Inclusion and interaction model]. Helsingin kaupunki [City of Helsinki]. Retrieved December 21, 2019, from https://www.hel.fi/helsinki/fi/kaupunki-ja-hallinto/osallistu-ja-vaikuta/vaikuttamiskanavat/osallisuus-ja-vuorovaikutusmalli/

IESE Business School. (2019). IESE Cities in Motion Index 2019. IESE Business School, University of Navarra. 10.15581/018.ST-509. Retrieved December 21, 2019, from https://media.iese.edu/research/pdfs/ST-0509-E.pdf

Kearney, A. T. (2019). A Question of Talent: How Human Capital Will Determine the Next Global Leaders: 2019 Global Cities Report. Retrieved December 15, 2019, from https://www.atkearney.com/documents/20152/2794549/A+Question+of+Talent%E2%80%942019+Global+Cities+Report.pdf/106f30b1-83db-25b3-2802-fa04343a36e4?t=1561389512018

Miller, J., & Parker, L. (2018, January 24). Open for Business: Strengthening the Economic Case. Retrieved December 19, 2019, from https://drive.google.com/file/d/1g7Al1vaxXCZDL27M6TLo3Q6L1iW1A0ii/view

Misra, T. (2018, April 25). The Most Inclusive U.S. Cities, Mapped. *CityLab.* Retrieved December 19, 2019, from https://www.citylab.com/equity/2018/04/the-most-inclusive-us-cities-mapped/558734/

Montagut, T., Vilà, G., & Riutort, S. (2016). Barcelona: A Citizen's Agreement for an Inclusive City. In T. Brandsen, S. Cattacin, A. Evers, & A. Zimmer (Eds.), *Social Innovations in the Urban Context. Nonprofit and Civil Society Studies.* Cham: Springer. https://doi.org/10.1007/978-3-319-21551-8_22

Nestpick. (2018). 2018 Millennial Cities Ranking. Retrieved December 19, 2019, from https://www.nestpick.com/millennial-city-ranking-2018/

OECD. (2016). *Making Cities Work for All: Data and Actions for Inclusive Growth.* Paris: OECD Publishing. https://doi.org/10.1787/9789264263260-en

Papadaki, M., & Kalogeraki, S. (2018). Exploring Social and Solidarity Economy (SSE) during the Greek Economic Crisis. *Partecipazione e conflitto, 11*(1), 38–69. https://doi.org/10.1285/i20356609v11iX1p38

Poethig, E., Greene, S., Stacy, C., Srini, T., & Meixell, B. (2018, April). Inclusive Recovery in US Cities. Research Report. Washington, D.C.: Urban Institute. Retrieved December 19, 2019, from https://www.urban.org/research/publication/inclusive-recovery-us-cities/view/full_report

Portland Development Commission. (n.d.). Strategic Plan 2015–2020. Retrieved December 20, 2019, from https://prosperportland.us/wp-content/uploads/2016/07/PDC-Strategic-Plan.pdf

Prosper Portland. (2019). Equity Framework. Retrieved December 20, 2019, from https://prosperportland.us/wp-content/uploads/2019/08/Equity-Framework-Booklet-web.pdf

Shafique, A., Antink, B., Clay, A., & Cox, E. (2019). *Inclusive Growth in Action: Snapshots of a New Economy.* London: Royal Society for the encouragement of Arts, Manufactures and Commerce (RSA). Retrieved December 7, 2019, from https://www.thersa.org/globalassets/pdfs/reports/rsa-inclusive-growth-in-action.pdf

URBACT. (n.d.). *Inclusive Entrepreneurship Model.* Barcelona/Spain. Website of URBACT. Retrieved July 22, 2020, from https://urbact.eu/inclusive-entrepreneurship-model

Whiton, J., & Muro, M. (2018, November 9). Eight of America's Most Digitally Inclusive Tech Cities. *Brookings*, Blog. Retrieved December 17, 2019, from https://www.brookings.edu/blog/the-avenue/2018/11/09/eight-of-americas-most-digitally-inclusive-tech-cities/

CHAPTER 8

Conclusion

Abstract The concluding chapter offers a recapitulation of the key insights generated in this volume. It highlights the positive role of economic inclusion in urban development. It is manifest in co-created and shared prosperity, which relies on resources, talent, and connections owned by various groups and individuals in the city. In short, economic inclusion should be given a high priority in the making of an inclusive city. Getting there requires broad stakeholder engagement in urban governance, an integrative and visionary approach to policymaking for inclusive city, and the valuing of varieties of capital, which is vital for the promotion of co-created and shared urban prosperity. The inclusive city is an urban development model for the twenty-first century that addresses pressing exclusion-related challenges and suggests responses conducive to balanced socio-economic development.

Keywords Economic inclusion • Social inclusion • Co-creation • Sharing • Urban prosperity • Governance • Leadership

ECONOMIC INCLUSION AS A KEY TO INCLUSIVE URBANITY

In this book, we have outlined the concept of the inclusive city and clarified its relevance to local economic development. Inclusion is a multidimensional concept to be understood in relation to its antithesis, exclusion.

A.-V. Anttiroiko, M. de Jong, *The Inclusive City*,
https://doi.org/10.1007/978-3-030-61365-5_8

Urban communities are circumscribed by various forms of exclusion that affect individuals and groups, and inclusion is the set of policy measures that aim at removing such exclusionary practices in order to promote fairness, equality, and prosperity within the given community. On the other hand, we also found that the absolute inclusion of everybody to everything is an illusory idea and that the public value of positive discrimination, exemption, or special rights granted to certain categories of people may affect other members of the community or even exclude them from what they desire. That is, trade-offs among the interest of various groups are sometimes required in any inclusive city.

We also hope to have demonstrated the importance of switching from a rights-oriented toward a value creation-oriented view of inclusion. The key idea underlying this book is that the *economic inclusion* of various societal segments, groups, and individuals in the creation of prosperity is a constructive and positive form of inclusion. It emphasizes the resources, talent, and potential people have rather than what they lack, and attaches value to what they have, which in a generative process—supported by the structures of the inclusive city—contributes to shared urban prosperity and ultimately to well-being of all members of the community. At the same time, this makes the power position of disadvantaged groups stronger when it comes to obtaining their fair share of the enhanced urban prosperity. It does its small part in combating economic polarization. In short, economic inclusion is a precondition for *co-created and shared prosperity*.

An economically inclusive city, by definition, refers to an urban community in which inclusion is an in-built element of the economy. Our discussion highlights two important aspects. First, we emphasize the need to take an analytical view of both the criteria of exclusion and the types of capital some groups are unjustly excluded from, which points to critical intersections that affect the conditions of value creation and the local economy as a whole. In addition, this view redirects attention from financial capital to other forms of capital, that is, cultural, social, physical, or natural capital. Second, we do not solely heed various scales of conventional businesses, but also to activities that emanate from associational, social, solidarity, sharing, and civic economies, which widens the view of value creation.

Ultimately, the inclusive economy invites all inhabitants to utilize their creative potential for the benefit of the entire community. This discussion directs our attention to the critical policy issues that puzzle local politicians, managers, and developers. Perhaps the most intriguing among them is: how to create favorable conditions for the emergence and further development of a socio-economically inclusive city?

BOTTOM-UP APPROACH TO ECONOMIC INCLUSION

Urban poverty and inequality have increased in the last two decades. There are clear segregation tendencies as a reflection of rising inequality, and even the middle class is struggling with their everyday life both in deteriorating and booming cities (Florida, 2017; Kotkin, 2014). This has set new challenges to urban development.

The most prevalent urban development concepts of our time, such as the smart city, in spite of its occasional environmental overtones, and the sustainable city, which seeks to embrace social, economic, and environmental agendas all at the same time, have their roots in techno-economic paradigm. A novel dimension, however, that appears to be taking off in the field of urban theory and practice is "the social," which is insufficiently addressed in the prevailing views of urban economic development. The inclusive city has become one of the catchwords, and potentially the central one, highlighting such social concerns. Yet, we wish to break away from a one-dimensional, rights-based social inclusion agenda by supplementing it with an economic value creation agenda. While our perspective emerges from widely shared criticism and skepticism of the formerly fashionable neoliberal city, this does not imply that we seek an alternative from the collectivist side of the ideological spectrum. Rather, we need to build on a sophisticated understanding of the dialectical relation between social and economic realities.

Our point of departure is an examination of the moral foundations of the economy. The neoliberal city, as we have learned to know it, creates wealth through market-oriented exploitation of and speculation around assets with a motivation primarily oriented toward profit and monetary gain at the expense of other values (Stiglitz, 2019; Mazzucato, 2018; Jacobs & Mazzucato, 2016; Roche & Jakub, 2017; Mayer, 2019). Such a bias urges us to look for alternative frameworks, which acknowledge that socio-economic structures can be designed to support the involvement of a greater variety of actors in the utilization of different types of capital, which are used to co-create value and generate dividends shared fairly by those involved in the process.

Inclusive urban development obviously does not aim at taking a U-turn to redistribution or collectivism in response to instability and injustice resulting from low taxes on the rich, deregulated labor and product markets, financialization, and the globalization of the economy. Rather, what is needed—beside obvious corrective macroeconomic policies—is an active role of local governments in encouraging and coordinating the involvement of various anchor institutions, civil society organizations, and large enterprises in the promotion of shared prosperity. When local organizations join forces, they have enough clout to activate and facilitate previously excluded segments of society and thus, through targeted support, contribute to the democratization of the economy.

Integrative and Synergistic Leadership

The issue of exclusion revolves around questions such as who is excluded from social and economic opportunities in our cities, how can these processes of exclusion be conceptualized, and how can we respond to it with balanced inclusionary policies. Exclusion is commonly associated with forms of racism, sexism, trans-/homophobia, classism, religism, ableism, and ageism. We wish to emphasize the need for a strategic approach to planning the inclusive city, including the creation of a sufficiently large knowledge base, taking a holistic approach, and designing and promoting integrative and synergistic policies. Popular as identity politics may be in the current academic and policy discourse, it clearly has a divisive edge to it, which should be carefully considered when building an inclusive city. Urban governments should show leadership and build a balanced and unifying framework, rather than become a handling center that passively deals with sectional interests. The ultimate goal should be to develop a unifying approach that provides everyone a fair opportunity (if not duty) to actively participate in value creation in an urban community using their own potential as well as in sharing the spoils derived from that. Groups in need of special support, such as disabled, must be addressed in the same fashion by positively looking at the talents and resources they do have rather than focusing only on what they miss or cannot perform. All this requires fair, value-based, and visionary leadership from urban governments and a sense of responsibility and entrepreneurship on the part of their public and private partners (cf. Hambleton, 2015).

We may picture this as a multilayered understanding of inclusive value creation, which begins with the fundamental preconditions for human dignity and basic material requirements, then evolves toward lower-level value-adding activities, and eventually develops further toward higher-level value creation through large-scale business enterprises (cf. Dahlvik, Franz, Hoekstra, & Kohlbacher, 2017). In concrete terms, strategies for urban value creation include activities such as providing access to skills and employment, supporting entrepreneurship and access to finance, and securing access to services that enhance economic opportunities (EBRD, 2017). Creating and sharing prosperity is best promoted by providing equal opportunities for all, incentivizing those who lack motivation, and enabling those who lack skills or abilities.

Such interventions require a keen perspective of currently existing forms of exclusion, the assessment of the missed opportunities for the creation of prosperity, and the design of combined efforts needed to include the bearers of these forgotten assets. There are many disadvantaged groups in any modern city unable or unwilling to harness their full potential in creating and capturing value. Their integration into value creation processes is thus a win-win game.

GOVERNANCE THROUGH NETWORKS, PARTNERSHIPS, AND PLATFORMS

Even justified and well-designed policies do not necessarily bring about good results, unless decision-making and service-delivery are properly governed and managed. We need institutional arrangements conducive to effective economic inclusion. Our starting point is that local government should not even try to promote inclusive prosperity by relying solely on its own resources, capacities, and policy programs. Rather, it is essential that all key stakeholders of the city are involved, most notably those who are supposed to benefit from such policies. In the same vain, relevant multi-level governance structures and resources should be tuned in to support such an urban transformation.

Given the imperative to involve and motivate different kinds of stakeholders in processes that require strong motivation and the absorption of various types of capitals, governance by hierarchies clearly will not do. The involvement of local actors bears fruit only if it allows for equal, flexible, mutually beneficial, and dynamically adjustable relations between them.

Organizational requirements of such processes are best met through networks, partnerships, and platforms. Citizen and stakeholder participation in economic inclusion should be partly fully open, partly selective, depending on the nature of the groups that are supported with particular inclusionary actions, programs, or regulations. Another vital aspect of participatory governance is the obvious need to turn attention to value co-creation, which presents a challenge to the institutions of public governance to find ways to help local stakeholders climb higher on the ladder of value creation. Each city will have its own geographic and institutional context and have acknowledged its own policy problems at hand; it should consequently flesh out the shape of its own inclusive city accordingly.

Inclusive City as a Model for the Twenty-First Century

It is good to keep in mind that eventually inclusion benefits us all. There is sufficient evidence to claim that the promotion of economic inclusion of disadvantaged and marginalized groups tends to improve the economic future of everyone in the city (Misra, 2018). Cities that suffer from deep ethnic, religious, linguistic, class-based, or age-based cleavages tend to be socially divided, economically underperforming, and politically tensional or even explosive. This is obviously not a viable path toward a sustainable future. Preventing such situations from arising and/or mitigating them when they already exist is a justification for a policy agenda for inclusive urban development. We may even claim that inclusive cities with structures that are conducive to balanced socio-economic development have the capacity to deal with many of the pressing challenges of the twenty-first century.

References

Dahlvik, J., Franz, Y., Hoekstra, M., & Kohlbacher, J. (2017). 3 Mechanisms of 'Success' or 'Failure' in Neighbourhood Initiatives. *ISR-Forschungsberichte, 46*, 36–43. https://doi.org/10.1553/ISR_FB046s36

EBRD. (2017). Economic Inclusion Strategy (EIS) 2017–2021. European Bank for Reconstruction and Development. Retrieved July 13, 2020, from https://www.ebrd.com/ebrd-economic-inclusion-strategy.pdf

Florida, R. (2017). *The New Urban Crisis: How Our Cities are Increasing Inequality, Deepening Segregation, and Failing the Middle Class—and What We Can Do About It*. New York, NY: Basic Books.

Hambleton, R. (2015). *Leading the Inclusive City: Place-based Innovation for a Bounded Planet.* Bristol, UK: Policy Press.

Jacobs, M., & Mazzucato, M. (Eds.). (2016). *Rethinking Capitalism: Economics and Policy for Sustainable and Inclusive Growth.* Chichester, UK: Wiley-Blackwell.

Kotkin, J. (2014). *The New Class Conflict.* Dagenham: Central Books.

Mayer, C. (2019). *Prosperity: Better Business Makes the Greater Good.* Illustrated Edition. Oxford: Oxford University Press.

Mazzucato, M. (2018). *The Value of Everything: Making and Taking in the Global Economy.* London: Allen Lane.

Misra, T. (2018, April 25). The Most Inclusive U.S. Cities, Mapped. *CityLab.* Retrieved December 19, 2019, from https://www.citylab.com/equity/2018/04/the-most-inclusive-us-cities-mapped/558734/

Roche, B., & Jakub, J. (2017). *Completing Capitalism: Heal Business to Heal the World.* Oakland, CA: Berrett Koehler Publishers.

Stiglitz, J. E. (2019). *People, Power and Profits: Progressive Capitalism for an Age of Discontent.* Allen Lane.

Printed by Printforce, the Netherlands